Real Life
Lessons For Teens

803 - 968

Real Life
Lessons For Teens

Practical Advice From A Former Teenager
Randy Simmons

GOSPEL
ADVOCATE
A TRUSTED NAME SINCE 1855

Gospel Advocate Company
P.O. Box 150, Nashville, Tennessee 37202

Published by Gospel Advocate Co.
P.O. Box 150, Nashville, TN 37202
http://www.gospeladvocate.com

ISBN: 0-89225-535-8

Dedication

To my wife, Dianne,
and my sons,
Scott and Matt

Contents

Introduction

In June 2001, I went on a senior retreat in the Everglades of South Florida with my congregation's 10 graduating high school seniors. My assigned task was to speak at the devotional. Most of these seniors I had known all their lives, and I cared deeply about their future. What could I say to motivate, inspire or encourage them?

I wrote a little devotional talk called, "Things I Wish I Had Known When I Graduated." I poured my heart out to them on spiritual and practical lessons I've learned in life but wish I had known at age 17! To make a long story short, my brief lesson led to a two-hour discussion and then a 13-week class that I called "Real Life Lessons For Teens."

In my first book, *Straight Talk for Teens*, we took a look at moral issues facing teenagers. In my second book, *What to Do When You Don't Know What to Do*, we discussed personal and emotional issues facing teenagers. My third book, *Basic Training: A Manual for Teens* focused on basic beliefs in Scripture that should be a part of every Christian teen's faith experience. And now, *Real Life Lessons for Teens* looks at practical truths learned in the school of life.

This book comes more from my heart than my head. My hope and my prayer is that it will in some small way be a tool the Lord uses to produce positive change in the heart, soul and mind of some of God's most precious creations – teens.

Flee the evil desires
of youth, and pursue
righteousness, faith,
love and peace,
along with those who
call on the Lord
out of a pure heart.

2 Timothy 2:22

Most of Us Are, At This Moment, What We Have Chosen to Be

In upstate New York, where the roads are long and sometimes a little rough, a sign reads, "Choose Your Rut Carefully, You'll Be in It for the Next 10 Miles!"

That sign is an accurate metaphor for life. All of us fall into habits or ruts in our lifestyles that define us. If you take a close look at your life right now, you will see that your life today is the result of the daily routines you have chosen over the past months and years.

- Are you succeeding at school? It didn't happen because one day last week you decided to start putting forth more effort. Your success is the result of daily decisions you have made during your school career.
- Are you 25 pounds overweight? It didn't happen because you ate a 25-pound pizza last week! Your weight gain has been an ongoing process for months, maybe even years.

Most things in your life that are working or not working are the result of your daily routine up to this point. Certainly other factors influence behavior such as environment or opportunity, but for the most part, most of us are what we have chosen or decided to be. Most of our "I can'ts" are really "I won'ts." We are not computers. We make choices and decisions, and those choices determine what we become.

This truth is actually good news because it means we can choose to make improvements in our lives. Romans 12:2 reads,

> Do not conform any longer to the pattern of this world, but be transformed by the renewing of your mind. Then you will be able to test and approve what God's will is – his good, pleasing and perfect will.

Do you realize the implications and the possibilities of that passage?

Transforming Your Mind

Several years ago the hottest toy in the country was "Transformers." These robots in disguise might appear to be a fire truck, a sports car, or some other item, but when you twisted them certain ways, they transformed into robots. The Bible says that can happen to our minds – they can be transformed! That means you may not be able to control all the circumstances of your life, but you can control your response. You can choose to turn your pain into profanity – or into poetry. You can take life's lemons and be a sour-face or you can make lemonade!

Do you want to be a victim or a victor? Before you answer, consider an important question Jesus once asked a disabled man in John 5:1-9:

> Some time later, Jesus went up to Jerusalem for a feast of the Jews. Now there is in Jerusalem near the Sheep Gate a pool, which in Aramaic is called Bethesda and which is surrounded by five covered colonnades. Here a great number of disabled people used to lie – the blind, the lame, the paralyzed. One who was there had been an invalid for thirty-eight years. When Jesus saw him lying there and learned that he had been in this condition for a long time, he asked him, "Do you want to get well?"

> "Sir," the invalid replied, "I have no one to help me into the pool when the water is stirred. While I am trying to get in, someone else goes down ahead of me."

> Then Jesus said to him, "Get up! Pick up your mat and walk." At once the man was cured; he picked up his mat and walked.

Jesus' question, "Do you want to get well?" sounds like an absurd question on the surface. Of course this man wanted to get well! You wouldn't ask a starving man, "Do you want food?" would you?

Actually, it was a very valid question, for there are people who, if given an opportunity for healing in their lives, might actually choose to remain sick. By staying a victim, they are free of some unpleasant responsibilities, and they gain sympathy and attention by complaining about their sickness. They can manipulate people by being sick or punish themselves if they feel guilty.

So when Jesus asked, "Do you want to get well?" He seems to be saying, "You have friends who bring you here and have developed relationships with others who come here frequently. You are accustomed to begging and gaining sympathy from others. If I heal you, your life will do a complete reversal. You'll be expected to get a job and become a giver instead of a taker, a victor instead of a victim. Are you ready for that change? Do you really want to get well?"

And Jesus would ask the same question of each of us.

How about you? Do you want to get well and transform your life? If so, consider these four biblical principles.

■ *Principle 1: Learn how to control your thoughts.* King Solomon wrote, "For as he thinketh in his heart, so is he" (Proverbs 23:7 KJV). In the New Testament, Paul wrote,

> Finally, brothers, whatever is true, whatever is noble, whatever is right, whatever is pure, whatever is lovely, whatever is admirable – if anything is excellent or praiseworthy – think about such things. Whatever you have learned or received or heard from me, or seen in me – put it into practice. And the God of peace will be with you (Philippians 4:8-9).

Here is a very important thought principle to remember:
Your mind controls your actions and emotions.
Your will controls your mind.
You control your will.
Therefore, you control your actions and emotions.

You choose your thoughts, and those thoughts, in turn, control your behavior and feelings. The reason the Bible is so insistent on your thinking about certain things and renewing your mind is because your mind and its thought processes are the very center of everything you become.

My brother is a pilot. Several years ago on a beautiful Sunday afternoon he took me up in his small Cessna plane for a leisurely ride. I asked him what would happen if he passed out or died because I couldn't fly the plane. He calmly replied, "We would both die." So I not so calmly replied, "Then teach me how to land this thing."

Almost instantly he took his hands off the controls and said, "It's all yours." I panicked! I wanted some control but not all of the control. I quickly replied, "Unless you are prepared to meet your God in a matter of moments, you better take control of this plane!"

My problem was he gave me control, and I didn't want it. A lot of people are like that about life. We don't really want to be responsible for having control, because we don't want to be ultimately responsible. But the truth is, we can't escape responsibility forever.

Benjamin Franklin once said, "With every right or privilege, there is a corresponding responsibility." The right of making your own choices or decisions is accompanied by the responsibility for those choices or decisions. You simply cannot avoid responsibility for what you think and what you do ... so choose your thoughts carefully and let the Lord help you learn how to control your thoughts.

■ *Principle 2: Decide to change.* I will never forget an experience I had one time counseling a 19-year-old girl who had developed a drug problem after months of casual usage. She told me about her friends' negative influence on her. She talked about a drug treatment center she had visited. She said she had tried everything she knew to stop using drugs but nothing was working. I sensed she was expecting me to jump in with some magic formula to help her, but instead I said, "Why don't you just choose to stop?"

She replied, "I can't."

To which I said, "What do you mean you can't? You make the choices. Nobody forces you. Nobody puts a gun to your head and makes you take drugs. Just choose to stop!"

She said, "You know, nobody ever put it to me that way."

You know what happened? She stopped. Because she chose to stop. Sometimes the best counsel is to just stop doing the things causing you trouble and choose to stop deliberately sinning and hurting yourself. I'm not minimizing the difficulty of breaking a serious drug addiction because that often requires professional help, but even then there must be a basic choice to stop, a decision to change.

God will help you change if you trust and obey Him. He is the God of the second chance. The Bible offers several examples of such changes, but a particularly fascinating one is recorded in 1 Corinthians 6:

> Do you not know that the wicked will not inherit the kingdom of God? Do not be deceived: Neither the sexually immoral nor idolators nor adulterers nor male prostitutes nor homosexual offenders nor thieves nor the greedy nor drunkards nor slanderers nor swindlers will inherit the kingdom of God. And that is what some of you were. But you were washed, you were sanctified, you were justified in the name of the Lord Jesus Christ and by the Spirit of our God (vv. 9-11).

Corinth was a wicked, first-century port city. People with every sort of sinful perversion and addiction lived there, and many were converted to Christ and changed by the Spirit of God. We, too, can change if we decide to change and be different from what we are now!

■ *Principle 3: Deal with some garbage from the past.* You don't get a clean slate just because you decide to make some personal improvements. There's still the stuff from yesterday to confront. Not with God – because with Him you do get a clean slate as He forgives you completely. But that doesn't change the fact that there is some garbage left over that you have to deal with. For example:

- If you've been arrested for drug possession and then repent, God will forgive you, but you still have to deal with the residue left over from your life of crime. You still have to face the law.
- If you committed sexual sin and were infected with a sexually transmitted disease, God will forgive you if you repent, but you still have to deal with the effects your actions left on your body.
- If you have been disobedient and disrespectful to godly parents and you repent of your sin and ask God to forgive you, He will, but you still have to deal with the hurt your actions have left on your relationship with your parents.
- If you decide to follow God's will for your life, God will help you, but you still have to endure the temptations your friends from the past toss your way.

Remember this – the Bible teaches there is a law of the harvest:

> Do not be deceived: God cannot be mocked. A man reaps what
> he sows. The one who sows to please his sinful nature, from that
> nature will reap destruction; the one who sows to please the
> Spirit, from the Spirit will reap eternal life (Galatians 6:7-8).

Your life today is the harvest of what you planted in the past. You are
reaping what you have sown in the past – both good and bad. When you
decide to make changes in your life, there is an adjustment period of
time where you have to deal with the garbage from yesterday.

Don't let the fact that you may still have some consequences to face
become an excuse for giving up. Remember the law of the harvest –
if you are now sowing good seed, you will eventually reap a good
harvest. So, "Let us not become weary in doing good, for at the proper time we will reap a harvest if we do not give up" (Galatians 6:9).

■ *Principle 4: Your choices affect your relationship with God.* Your
relationship with God is your most important relationship. It will matter 100 years from now and 1,000,000 years from now. After all, what
you choose concerning your relationship with God will determine
your eternal destiny.

Jesus once asked His disciples two life-changing questions:

> What good will it be for a man if he gains the whole world, yet
> forfeits his soul? Or what can a man give in exchange for his
> soul? (Matthew 16:26).

Of course, the answer to both questions is a resounding "Nothing!"
Our eternal salvation should always be number one on our priority list.

I Have Learned That...

My mind wanders back to so many nights under the moon, sitting at a campfire, singing, "I have decided to follow Jesus, no turning back, no turning back." I am so glad I decided, I chose, to follow Jesus because it is the most important choice of all. In fact, I have never met a single person who decided to follow Jesus and regretted the decision.

How about you? Have you decided to follow Jesus? What you decide will determine your eternal destiny. Choose wisely and carefully because I have learned that most of us are, at this moment, what we have chosen to be.

Talking Back

1. What are the ruts or routines in your life right now? Are they having a positive or negative influence on you?

2. Do you agree that most of our "I can'ts" are really "I won'ts"?

3. Discuss the implications of Jesus' question, "Do you want to get well?"

4. What does Benjamin Franklin's statement, "With every right or privilege, there is a corresponding responsibility," mean to you?

5. How is life like a harvest?

Exercising Your Faith

1. Make a list of positive changes you would like to make in your life. Put the list beside your bed and pray every morning and night for God to help you make the changes.

2. Commit to memory the thought principle in the lesson:
   Your mind controls your actions and emotions.
   Your will controls your mind.
   You control your will.
   Therefore, you can control your actions and emotions.

People Should Worry Less And Pray More

For 15 years a wife bothered her husband nearly every night by awakening him: "Honey, wake up! I think I hear a burglar in the house!"

Almost every night the devoted husband would stumble downstairs, look around, and return to bed, reassuring his wife, "No burglar."

But one night was different. The husband actually found a thief in the dining room, stealing their valuables. He politely asked the burglar, "Before you finish packing up our family silver, would you mind coming upstairs with me? There's someone upstairs who has been waiting 15 years to meet you!"

That wife may have lost some valuable possessions that night, but she had been the victim of a far worse criminal for 15 years – worry!

I must confess that for much of my life I have been something of a worrywart. And, as a minister, I've counseled with hundreds of people who have worried themselves into physical, emotional or mental weariness. But I must also confess that worrying has never improved my life in any way, nor have I ever known anyone who profited from worry or anxiety.

The great author and humorist, Mark Twain, once said, "I am an old man and have known many troubles, but most of them never happened." Twain was right, and numerous studies have shown that most of the things we worry about are not legitimate worries.

A study at the University of Wisconsin by Margaret McCordie concluded:

- 40 percent of the things we worry about never happen;
- 30 percent of our worrying is about things over and past that cannot be changed;
- 10 percent are petty worries;
- 12 percent are unnecessary health worries;
- 8 percent are legitimate worries.

The Three Categories of Worry

Most worries can be reduced to three categories:

■ *Things that have already happened.* What possible good can come from worrying about things in the past? Mistakes from the past cannot be re-lived. So, take Paul's advice and forget those things that are behind (Philippians 3:13).

■ *Things that are going to happen and are beyond our control.* Again, what possible good can come from worrying about things one cannot control?

■ *Things that may never happen.* This is the most worthless kind of worry and yet it is the most common. Sociological studies have repeatedly found that nearly half the things we worry about never happen.

Basically, there are two things we should never worry about:

- Things you can change.
- Things you can't change.

Why worry about something you can change; just change it and you won't have to worry about it. And why worry about something you can't change? If you cannot change it, why worry about it? Isn't that logical? It's also biblical! Consider what Jesus said about worry:

> Therefore I tell you, do not worry about your life, what you will eat or drink; or about your body, what you will wear. Is not life more important than food, and the body more important than clothes? Look at the birds of the air; they do not sow or reap or store away in barns, and yet your heavenly Father feeds them. Are you not much more valuable than they? Who of you by worrying can add a single hour to his life?

And why do you worry about clothes? See how the lilies of the field grow. They do not labor or spin. Yet I tell you that not even Solomon in all his splendor was dressed like one of these. If that is how God clothes the grass of the field, which is here today and tomorrow is thrown into the fire, will he not much more clothe you, O you of little faith?

So do not worry, saying, "What shall we eat?" or "What shall we drink?" or "What shall we wear?" For the pagans run after all these things, and your heavenly Father knows that you need them. But seek first his kingdom and his righteousness, and all these things will be given to you as well. Therefore do not worry about tomorrow, for tomorrow will worry about itself. Each day has enough trouble of its own (Matthew 6:25-34).

Worries Are the Same Yesterday and Today

The circumstances of life may change but people never do. Worry is a proof of that because Jesus points out that people worried about the same things 2,000 years ago that they worry about today:

■ *Food.* "Do not worry about ... what you will eat or drink." Some people today worry about where their next meal will come from, and some people today worry they will eat too much at their next meal!

■ *Fashion.* "And why do you worry about clothes? See how the lilies of the field grow. They do not labor or spin." People are so worried about being fashionable these days. We want to make sure we have the right name brands, the right labels and the right shoes.

■ *Future.* "[D]o not worry about tomorrow, for tomorrow will worry about itself. Each day has enough trouble of its own." Someone once said, "Worry is the interest we pay in advance today for trouble that may never come tomorrow."

■ *Finances.* "Do not store up for yourselves treasures on earth, where moth and rust destroy, where thieves break in and steal. But store up for yourselves treasures in heaven, where moth and rust do not destroy, and where thieves do not break in and steal. For where your treasure is, there your heart will be also" (Matthew 6:19-21). Every time the stock market drops, some people worry themselves into a frenzy.

If you look carefully at the things Jesus said we tend to worry about, you will find two common denominators: none of them have eternal importance, and all of them say to God, in effect, "God, you cannot be trusted. You cannot handle my needs."

We are like the cow in the poem, "The Worry Cow":

> The worry cow would have lived 'til now
> If she hadn't lost her breath.
> But she thought her hay wouldn't last all day,
> So she mooed herself to death.

Have I convinced you that worry is useless? Not only should people worry less, but they should also pray and trust God more. Why worry when we can pray? Consider what the Bible says:

> Cast all your anxiety on him because he cares for you (1 Peter 5:7).

> Do not be anxious about anything, but in everything, by prayer and petition, with thanksgiving, present your requests to God. And the peace of God, which transcends all understanding, will guard your hearts and your minds in Christ Jesus (Philippians 4:6-7).

How to Worry Less and Pray More

How do we learn not to be "anxious about anything" but to worry less and pray more? Here are five suggestions:

■ *Recognize that worry is a waste of time.* Jesus' question, "Who of you by worrying can add a single hour to his life?" puts anxiety in perspective for us. Worrying never solved a problem, never dried a tear, never removed an obstacle. Worry has never made bad things good or good things better.

Worrying is like cultivating and watering ground where you haven't planted any seed. You've wasted water, time and energy, and you still have nothing to show for your efforts. Worry is a waste of time.

■ *Trust God to take care of your needs.* Jesus said, "[D]o not worry, saying, 'What shall we eat?' or 'What shall we drink?' or 'What shall we wear?' For the pagans run after all these things, and your heavenly Father knows that you need them. But seek first his kingdom and his righteousness, and all these things will be given to you as well"

(Matthew 6:31-33). God has promised to take care of us – that's His job. It's our job to let Him!

Worry puts us on the same level as a "pagan," a non-believer. So, when we worry, we are not acting like a child of God, but like an unbeliever.

Trusting God to take care of us means that we have to eliminate phrases from our conversation such as, "I just don't think I can make it" or "I don't think there is any way I can hold up." You can hold up. You can make it. If you trust God to take care of you, and seek Him first, He will take care of you.

■ *Make sure you put Jesus first in your life.* A prerequisite to having your needs met by God is to seek first His kingdom and His righteousness. In today's world it can be very difficult to make the Lord priority number one.

All too often we are like the young boy who was driving a big hayrack down the road and it turned over right in front of a farmer's house. The farmer came out and saw the young boy crying and said, "Son, don't worry about this, we can fix it. Right now, dinner's ready. Why don't you come in and eat with us and then I'll help you put the hay back on the rack."

"No, I can't. My father is going to be very angry with me."

The farmer replied, "Now don't argue, just come in and have some dinner and you'll feel better."

"I'm just afraid my father is going to be very angry with me," the boy said again.

The farmer and the young boy went inside and had dinner. Afterward, as they walked outside to the hayrack, the farmer said, "Well, don't you feel better now?"

"Not really," the boy said. "I just know that my father will be very angry with me."

"Nonsense," the farmer said. "Where is your father anyway?"

"He's under that pile of hay," the boy answered.

If we are going to win over worry, we have to be sure we take God from under the pile of hay where we sometimes try to keep Him, and seek Him first.

■ *Determine to live one day at a time.* "[D]o not worry about tomorrow, for tomorrow will worry about itself. Each day has enough trouble of its own" (Matthew 6:34).

People who worry too much about the future cannot possibly enjoy the present. Devote your energy to living for the Lord today and trusting God about your tomorrows. Psalm 118:24 is a wonderful truth about living for today: "This is the day the Lord has made; let us rejoice and be glad in it." As we rejoice and are happy in the blessings of today, we will find the worries of tomorrow melt away.

■ *Pray your problems and worries away.* Whenever you start to worry, one question should immediately pop into your mind: Have I prayed about this? Philippians 4:6 gives a three-step formula for praying instead of worrying:

1. Do not be anxious about anything. Make a choice that you are not going to worry or be anxious.
2. Pray about everything. Talk to God specifically about everything. Give your worries to the only One who truly can do something about them.
3. Pray with thanksgiving. Nothing changes your attitude like gratitude! Count your blessings instead of your worries.

A ship was sailing from Liverpool, England, to New York City. The captain of the ship had his family with him. The ship encountered a terrible storm in the middle of the night. The captain's 8-year-old daughter was on her first trip and was awakened by the storm. Frightened, she asked her mother, "What's wrong?" Her mother told her they were in a terrible storm.

The little girl asked, "Is father on deck?"

"Yes, father is on deck," her mother replied. The little girl returned to her bed and went right back to sleep.

Our heavenly Father is always on deck. The message of the Bible is when the worries of life swirl around us like a vicious storm, we can be sure our Father is on deck protecting us.

I Have Learned That...

We only have two choices – we can worry or we can pray. Worrying reduces praying, and praying reduces worrying. I've done both and I've learned this: People should worry less and pray more!

Talking Back

1. Why do you think people worry? Why do you worry?

2. In the Sermon on the Mount, Jesus pointed out four primary things people worry about – food, fashion, future and finances. Which of these tempt you to worry?

3. Do you think God takes your prayers seriously? Why or why not?

4. What hinders people from trusting God to take care of their needs?

5. Discuss the phrase, "Worrying reduces praying, and praying reduces worrying."

Exercising Your Faith

1. Make a list of everything you worry about in your life. After making the list, categorize it into one of these categories:
   • Things that have already happened.
   • Things that are going to happen and are beyond my control.
   • Things that may never happen.

   What was the breakdown of your list? Remind yourself not to worry about something you can change; just change it. Remind yourself not to worry about something you can't change. If you can't change it, what good does it do to worry about it?

2. When you find yourself worrying instead of praying, put a rubber band around your wrist to remind yourself to ask the question, "Have I prayed about this?" Then pray!

Forgiveness Is Much Better Than Bitterness

I was riding along in my car, windows down, sunroof open, relaxing and listening to music on the radio when suddenly the words of a song by Don Henley caught my attention and sent my mind into overdrive. Although I was vaguely familiar with the song, "The Heart of the Matter," I didn't know all the words so I promptly pulled into a music store and bought the CD so I could hear it again. The verse that caught my attention was about the anger we feel toward people in our lives who let us down and hurt us and about the importance of forgiveness.

It is a fact of life that we will get hurt. The question is not if we'll get hurt; it's when we'll get hurt. The bigger issue is what we will do when we get hurt. We will get either better or bitter. I've learned that forgiveness is much better than bitterness.

The Bible tells us that a bitter heart is a bad heart and will cause us trouble:

> Make every effort to live in peace with all men and to be holy; without holiness no one will see the Lord. See to it that no one misses the grace of God and that no bitter root grows up to cause trouble and defile many (Hebrews 12:14-15).

Bitterness is described as a root. A root is beneath the surface, invisible to the eye, but doing its work in the soil, producing either a productive plant or a wasteful weed. Likewise the root of bitterness reaches deep into the soil of one's heart, and although often invisible to others, it gives birth to pain and misery.

We become bitter for basically one of two reasons: what is done to us or what is said about us.

How to Handle the Hurt

How do we handle our hurts so that they don't deteriorate into a root of bitterness? Basically, we only have three choices:

■ *We can repress the hurt.* Some people bury their hurt deep inside themselves. On the surface, they act as if nothing has happened, but that invisible root of bitterness is slowly at work in their hearts, and at some point it rises up through anger, loneliness or depression.

■ *We can express the hurt.* A news story heard in Liberal, Kan., told of an elderly lady driving a big expensive car. As she was preparing to back into a parallel parking space, a young man in a small sports car zoomed into the space ahead of her. The lady angrily asked why he had done that when he could clearly tell that she was trying to park there. His response was, "Because I'm young, and I'm quick." When he came back to his car a few minutes later, he found the elderly lady using her big, expensive car as a battering ram backing up and then ramming into his car. He ran up to her and angrily asked why she was wrecking his car. Her response was, "Because I'm old, and I'm rich!"

When we are hurt, it is tempting to scream, blow up and get it out of your system. And it may even make you feel better – for just a moment. But it usually hurts the person on whom you vented and later causes you regret and guilt.

Often people repress their hurt feelings for a little while and then they explode and express their hurt feelings in a negative way. It becomes a vicious cycle of repressing and expressing as the root of bitterness is never dug up and just grows uncontrolled into rage and abuse. There is a better way.

■ *We can confess our hurt and forgive those who hurt us.* Confessing that we are hurt helps us avoid repressing our feelings and is the first step toward forgiving the offender.

We have a role model of One who practiced this kind of forgiveness.

He was falsely arrested. He was convicted in a rigged trial and sentenced to die in a cruel way – crucifixion. Before being crucified He was beaten nearly to death. He was mocked and spat upon. And then, when the soldiers drove nails into His hands and feet, His response was, "Father, forgive them, for they do not know what they are doing" (Luke 23:34).

His name was Jesus Christ.

Choosing Forgiveness Over Bitterness

Jesus was practicing what He had preached. In Luke 15:11-32, He told a story about a son who broke his relationship with his father and then wanted to repair it. Then he told how the father chose forgiveness over bitterness:

Jesus continued: "There was a man who had two sons. The younger one said to his father, 'Father, give me my share of the estate.' So he divided his property between them.

Not long after that, the younger son got together all he had, set off for a distant country and there squandered his wealth in wild living. After he had spent everything, there was a severe famine in that whole country, and he began to be in need. So he went and hired himself out to a citizen of that country, who sent him to his fields to feed pigs. He longed to fill his stomach with the pods that the pigs were eating, but no one gave him anything.

When he came to his senses, he said, 'How many of my father's hired men have food to spare, and here I am starving to death! I will set out and go back to my father and say to him: Father, I have sinned against heaven and against you. I am no longer worthy to be called your son; make me like one of your hired men.' So he got up and went to his father.

But while he was still a long way off, his father saw him and was filled with compassion for him; he ran to his son, threw his arms around him and kissed him.

The son said to him, 'Father, I have sinned against heaven and against you. I am no longer worthy to be called your son.'

But the father said to his servants, 'Quick! Bring the best robe and put it on him. Put a ring on his finger and sandals on his feet. Bring the fattened calf and kill it. Let's have a feast and celebrate. For this son of mine was dead and is alive again; he was lost and is found.' So they began to celebrate.

Meanwhile, the older son was in the field. When he came near the house, he heard music and dancing. So he called one of the servants and asked him what was going on. 'Your brother has come,' he replied, 'and your father has killed the fattened calf because he has him back safe and sound.'

The older brother became angry and refused to go in. So his father went out and pleaded with him. But he answered his father, 'Look! All these years I've been slaving for you and never disobeyed your orders. Yet you never gave me even a young goat so I could celebrate with my friends. But when this son of yours who has squandered your property with prostitutes comes home, you kill the fattened calf for him!'

'My son,' the father said, 'you are always with me, and everything I have is yours. But we had to celebrate and be glad, because this brother of yours was dead and is alive again; he was lost and is found.' "

The son said to his father, in effect, "I want my freedom. I want to do my own thing and I don't really care what anyone else says or thinks." This attitude is typical of so many people today. The son made his choice, hurt his family and went away to squander his inheritance in wild living. He left his family, lost his self-respect, caused major heartache, and ended up in the pigpen, literally.

Seeking Forgiveness

Can such deep hurt be repaired without bitterness? Yes! The relationship between son and father was healed when the son took several difficult, but necessary actions:

■ *He realized what he had done.* "[H]e came to his senses." The first step to reconciliation of a relationship is to stop playing the blame game and accept responsibility. Recognize if you have hurt someone and start on the road toward repentance and forgiveness.

■ *He resolved to return home with a humble spirit.* "I will set out and go back to my father. ... 'Father, I have sinned against heaven and against you. I am no longer worthy to be called your son; make me like one of your hired men.' " The son decided to do something to repair the hurt. If you do nothing, nothing will be repaired. Look carefully at those words, "make me." You repair a hurt relationship by moving from "give me" (Luke 15:12) to "make me" (v. 19).

■ *The father accepted the son back with open arms and forgave him.* What are we to do for others who have hurt us but seek to repair the hurt? Lay aside any bitterness and forgive! In fact, we are never more like the Lord than when we forgive a person who hurt us.

■ *The father and son celebrated the reconciliation of their relationship.* It is an occasion for celebration and rejoicing every time a hurt is healed and a fault is forgiven!

Giving in to Bitterness

But, unfortunately, a third party in this story shows us the opposite of forgiveness – bitterness.

The whole town was celebrating a homecoming except for one person, the older brother. He stood outside the house, bitter and angry, refusing even to go inside. Notice what such bitterness will do:

■ *He didn't treat his father with respect.* He challenged his father's decisions and, furthermore, forced the father to come outside and talk to him, certainly a source of embarrassment and disrespect.

■ *He questioned his father's generosity.* "[Y]ou never gave me even a young goat so I could celebrate with my friends." Bitterness leads to jealousy and resentment.

■ *He spoke of his father like an employer.* "All these years I've been slaving for you." Instead of being grateful for what he had, he was ungrateful because of what he didn't have. On the surface he appeared to be loyal and an obedient son and worker, but deep in his heart a root of bitterness was developing.

■ *He was unforgiving toward his brother, not even claiming him as his brother.* Did you notice he said, "[W]hen this son of yours," not "when this brother of mine"? He didn't learn that spiteful spirit from his father. Bitterness is caused by Satan in order to build walls instead of bridges.

One of the sad consequences of bitterness is that it grows like a cancer silently within us until it poisons us, making us unable to forgive and reach out to others in love and receive love in return. After all, you have to experience forgiveness before you can share forgiveness.

How can we forgive and be better rather than bitter?

Forget the Hurt

Whatever caused the problem that planted the root of bitterness in your heart must be put behind you.

> Get rid of all bitterness, rage and anger, brawling and slander, along with every form of malice. Be kind and compassionate to one another, forgiving each other, just as in Christ God forgave you (Ephesians 4:31-32).

In his biography of Confederate General Robert E. Lee, *The Last Years*, author Charles Flood tells a story about the great general visiting a lady in Virginia shortly after the Civil War ended. She was filled with hatred and bitterness toward the Union. When he asked her why, she took him out in her front yard and showed him the remains of a beautiful old tree that had been like a family heirloom. During a raid on her home the Union army had shot most of the limbs off the tree and carved their initials on the trunk, destroying its beauty.

She looked at Lee and asked, "What do you think I ought to do about that?" After a moment of silent thought, Lee replied, "My dear Madam, I think you ought to cut it down and forget it."

Whatever it was that hurt you and left you with a root of bitterness, get rid of it. Cut down the tree, remove the root, and forget the hurt.

Forgive the Person

Whoever caused bitterness to grow like a malignant tumor in your heart needs to be forgiven. If you don't, you will miss the grace of God. "See to it that no one misses the grace of God and that no bitter root grows up to cause trouble and defile many" (Hebrews 12:15).

That's what grace is all about – forgiving others who have done you wrong just as God forgives us when we do wrong. Everyone wins when we forgive rather than hold on to bitterness.

Free Your Spirit

One of the great paradoxes of life is that forgiveness often does more for the forgiver than the forgiven. Forgiving others is difficult work. C.S. Lewis put it well, "Forgiveness is a beautiful word until you actually have something to forgive." Because it is such hard work, you may be wondering, "What's in it for me?" This is what's in it for you – a free spirit healed from the root of bitterness!

You have probably used the phrase TGIF. Well, I think you should continue to use it, but not as we know it, "Thank God, It's Friday." Instead, let it be a reminder of your relationship with God and others. Let it remind you to pray, "Thank God, I'm Forgiven." And let it remind you to say, "Thank God, I Forgive."

I Have Learned That...

Don Henley was right; the heart of the matter really is forgiveness. And I've learned that forgiveness is much better than bitterness.

Talking Back

1. How will anger and unforgiveness "eat you up inside."

2. Answer honestly, how do you handle hurt most often: by repressing it, expressing it, or confessing it and forgiving?

3. Contrast the attitude of the father and the older brother in the parable of the prodigal son. Which one are you most like?

4. Do you think it is necessary to experience forgiveness before you can share forgiveness? Why or why not?

5. Do you struggle more with the "whatever" or the "whoever" of forgiveness?

Exercising Your Faith

1. Discuss Don Henley's song "The Heart of the Matter" with someone you have been separated from by unforgiveness or bitterness and offer to reconcile the relationship.

2. In a prominent place you view every day, put the acronym TGIF to remind you "Thank God, I'm forgiven" and "Thank God, I forgive."

Heroes and Role Models Should Be Carefully Chosen

Most kids have heroes during their childhood and adolescence; I was no exception. I can still see the hero of my youth in my mind's eye looking exactly as he did in the 1960s. A pin-striped New York Yankee uniform with No. 7 on the back, a strong, athletic body and a boyish grin described "The Mick."

Mickey Mantle had a freakish combination of power and speed. He hit the longest homeruns anyone had ever seen (and as a switch-hitter, from both sides of the plate) and was at the same time the fastest runner in baseball. He led the Yankees to 12 World Series. And he was Hollywood handsome.

He was my hero and a hero to millions of baseball-loving kids who grew up in the 1950s and '60s. For a variety of reasons that no dry recitation of the statistics can possibly capture, he was the most compelling baseball hero of the last half of the 20th century.

But there was a lot we didn't know about "The Mick" in those days. Heavy drinking scarred his soul and destroyed his liver. Multiple affairs tarnished his family life. As those revelations slowly surfaced, many of us who had admired Mantle no longer viewed him as a role model.

Then came the summer of 1995 when Mantle's lifestyle caught up with him. He needed a liver transplant. At this point, Mantle finally began to accept and appreciate the distinction between a role model and a hero. The first he never had been; the second he could still be. Shortly after his transplant he spoke these words at a press conference, words that would be printed on the "Join Mickey's Team" organ donor card:

> The best gift I ever got was on June 8, 1995, when an organ donor gave me and five other patients at Baylor University Medical Center in Dallas the organs we needed to live. I guess you could say I got another time at bat.
>
> Now I want to give something back. I can do that first by telling kids and parents to take care of their bodies. Don't drink or do drugs. Your health is the main thing you've got, so don't blow it.
>
> Second, think hard about being an organ and tissue donor if the time ever comes. Sign this card, carry it with you, and let your family know how you feel.
>
> Thanks for your prayers and kindness. I'll never be able to make up all I owe God and the American people. But if you will join me in supporting the cause of organ and tissue donation, it would be a great start.

Because of his courageous example, organ donations went up 30 percent across America and thousands of lives were saved or improved.

Mantle died two months later, but our last memories of "The Mick" are more heroic than the first. After all, we all sin and make mistakes, and we would not want to be held accountable for every moment of our lives without grace and forgiveness.

Who Are Your Heroes?

Researchers for the *World Almanac and Book of Facts* asked 2,000 American eighth-grade students to name people they admired and wanted to be like. Nearly all the answers were entertainers or athletes, the Mickey Mantles of your generation – until Sept. 11, 2001.

Sept. 11 changed everything for most of us.

We know the major facts. There were two big buildings and more than 4,000 people at 8:48 a.m. in New York City. It seemed like a normal Tuesday morning. Just an hour later the buildings and the people were gone, victims of an unspeakable terrorist attack. More than 2,000 people dead in the burning, collapsing buildings and among them were more than 300 firemen.

Wait a minute! Three hundred firemen? This is the part that boggles your mind and redefines your image of a hero. Nearly all of the dead were in the World Trade Center Twin Towers – working at their desks, maintenance workers, visitors or service employees. They were there when the planes struck the Towers. But the 300 firemen were not there; they went there.

They ran into the burning buildings, not out, and ran up the stairs, not down, to save lives. And save lives they did – thousands were carried out or directed out by the brave firemen. They brought love into a story about hate because only love will make you enter fire.

And they did something else: They redefined the word "hero" for most Americans. Talent in a sport, the arts or entertainment was no longer a sufficient definition for "hero." Courage, bravery, strength, character and sacrifice were the new defining characteristics of a new hero.

The lingering mental images of Sept. 11 are those of common men and women who displayed uncommon strength of mind, body and soul:

■ The New York City Fire and Police Department;

■ The passengers and employees on the planes that crashed into the Twin Towers, the Pentagon, and the field in Pennsylvania. Heroic action by the passengers in the Pennsylvania crash prevented another catastrophic crash in Washington, D.C.;

■ The three firemen in New York City who raised the flag at "Ground Zero" just hours after the disaster, inspiring millions to keep a strong spirit. *The New York Post* ran a picture of the flag raisers on the front page with the headline "Proof Through the Night That Our Flag Was Still There";

■ The millions of Americans who went to New York as volunteers to serve the rescue workers or gave blood or money;

■ The American military servicemen and servicewomen who put their lives in danger to protect our freedoms and sought to bring the terrorists to justice.

We will have role models and heroes. Sept. 11 taught us we should choose our heroes carefully. Let me suggest some heroes for you to consider.

Parents

Nobody is perfect and certainly parents make mistakes. But if you have parents who love you, provide for you, protect you, support you and try to bring you up "in the training and instruction of the Lord" (Ephesians 6:4), they are worthy of being your heroes.

Reader's Digest (April 1995) told a beautiful story about a young man who considered his dad to be his hero. The story happened at the Baseball Hall of Fame in Cooperstown, N.Y.

They were renovating the Hall of Fame museum, which included putting in a new state-of-the-art humidification system to better protect and preserve those historic items that honor and celebrate the greatest baseball players of all time. They removed all the displays from the second floor exhibit area while the refurbishing work was being done. One of the workers found a picture underneath one of the display cases. The picture was that of a man in a 1940s-style baseball uniform. He had a bat on his right shoulder. On his left sleeve, there was the emblem of a small dinosaur.

The picture was taken to Ted Spencer, curator of the museum. Spencer knew immediately that the man in the picture was not one of the 216 baseball giants honored in the Hall of Fame. Who was he? How did the picture get there? Spencer guessed that the uniform was probably from some industrial league team and, because of the dinosaur logo, was likely sponsored by the Sinclair Refining Company. Turning the picture over, he found no name, but there was a short message on the back written by the man's son.

The curator was fascinated by the small mystery, so he sent a copy of the photo to his friend, Steve Wolf, at *Sports Illustrated*. They ran the picture, and before long the truth came out. The baseball player in the picture was a man named Joe O'Donnell. His son, Pat, had hidden the picture of his dad under the display case. Why? Because he wanted to put his dad in the Baseball Hall of Fame after his dad had died. The message on the back of the picture says this:

> You were never too tired to play catch. On your days off you helped build the Little League field. You always came to watch me play. You were a Hall of Fame dad. I wish I could share this moment with you. Your son, Pat.

In August 1989, Pat O'Donnell had toured the Baseball Hall of Fame. He noticed a small opening between the bottom of the display case and the floor, and when no one was looking, he slid the photo of his dad beneath the case. He said aloud while he was putting it under the case: "Now you're in the Hall of Fame, Dad. This is where the best of the best get to go. And you're the best of the best."

In the fall 1994, Spencer put Joe O'Donnell's photo in an envelope. He enclosed a letter explaining the situation and addressed the letter to any future curator who might find the envelope. He then put the envelope back under the display case where Pat had originally hidden the photograph of his dad. This gave Joe O'Donnell a permanent place in the Baseball Hall of Fame.

Teachers, Coaches and Spiritual Leaders

Teachers sacrifice for students. They endure low pay, criticism and discipline problems for the sake of teaching important facts, values and principles that students need to become productive in life.

Coaches and instructors instill discipline and the value of teamwork while teaching us how to play a sport or play a musical instrument or perform an art. The harder they are on us at the time, the more we respect them as the years go by.

Elders, preachers, Bible teachers and other people who are spiritual leaders play a vital role in our lives. They have taken on an important role for which they themselves will be judged: "Not many of you should presume to be teachers, my brothers, because you know that we who teach will be judged more strictly" (James 3:1).

If spiritual leaders are doing their best to help us grow in Christ, they should be respected and honored: "The elders who direct the affairs of the church well are worthy of double honor, especially those whose work is preaching and teaching" (1 Timothy 5:17).

Biblical Heroes

A few years ago, I took my sons to Washington, D.C. We visited all the major attractions in the capital, but one that stands out in my memory was a visit to Arlington National Cemetery. This cemetery, the most famous in America, covers 612 acres and contains the bodies of many of our nation's finest heroes. The ceremony with the changing of the guard at the tomb of unknown soldiers from World Wars I and II, the Korean War, and the Vietnam War is dignified and emotion-filled. The grave of President John F. Kennedy, marked by an "eternal flame," lies on a hillside in the cemetery. It is a moving place to visit, sacred ground where the faithful heroes of our country are remembered.

God has provided for us a "Hall of Fame of Faith" in Hebrews 11, a place where we can remember biblical heroes as they teach us that the way to live victoriously is to live by faith. Here are just a few of those mentioned in the chapter.

■ "By faith Noah, when warned about things not yet seen, in holy fear built an ark to save his family" (Hebrews 11:7). Think of how ridiculous the building project of an ark must have seemed to his neighbors. The ark was a thousand times too big for his family, being about twice the length of a football field and four stories high. And to make what Noah was doing seem all the more ridiculous, it took more than 100 years to build! Yet, Noah acted in faith, believing God's Word about a coming catastrophic flood rather than the public opinion polls or the conventional wisdom of the day.

■ "By faith Abraham, when called to go to a place he would later receive as his inheritance, obeyed and went, even though he did not know where he was going" (Hebrews 11:8). Usually, when we move, we know where we are going, how we will get there, and how long it will take. But when Abraham and Sarah said goodbye to their family and friends, they left no forwarding address. By faith, they followed God's plan for their lives although only God knew what was in store for them.

■ "By faith Moses, when he was grown, refused to be known as the son of Pharaoh's daughter. He chose to be mistreated along with the people of God rather than to enjoy the pleasures of sin for a short time" (Hebrews 11:24-25). Moses was in position to enjoy everything Egypt had to offer, being raised as the son of Pharaoh's daughter. Seeing the mistreatment of his own people, the Jews, he had to decide between becoming pampered Egyptian royalty or joining the cause of his own people. When he made his choice, he knew he would be entering a life of suffering and difficulty. By faith, he did the right thing rather than the convenient thing, denying himself the "pleasures of sin for a short time." God, in time, honored his choice by making him the leader who helped free the Jewish people from Egyptian slavery.

■ "Others were tortured and refused to be released, so that they might gain a better resurrection. Some faced jeers and flogging, while still others were chained and put in prison. They were stoned; they were sawed in two; they were put to death by the sword. They went about in sheepskins and goatskins, destitute, persecuted and mistreated – the world was not worthy of them. They wandered in deserts and mountains, and in caves and holes in the ground. These were all commended for their faith, yet none of them received what had been promised. God had planned something better for us so that only together with us would they be made perfect" (Hebrews 11:35-40).

The vocabulary of the closing verses of "God's Hall of Fame of Faith" is painful to read: "tortured … jeers and flogging … chains and prisons … stoned … sawed in two … ." The church in America has been protected from this kind of persecution. We must be mindful of the fact that others around the world, even today, still have to endure such mistreatment for their Christian faith. They are true spiritual heroes.

The Ultimate Hero

Hebrews 12 continues the list of heroes of faith, including the greatest Champion of faith, the ultimate hero, Jesus Christ:

> Therefore, since we are surrounded by such a great cloud of witnesses, let us throw off everything that hinders and the sin that so easily entangles, and let us run with perseverance the race marked out for us. Let us fix our eyes on Jesus, the author and perfecter of our faith, who for the joy set before him endured the cross, scorning its shame, and sat down at the right hand of the throne of God. Consider him who endured such opposition from sinful men, so that you will not grow weary and lose heart (vv. 1-3).

When earthly heroes fail us, as they inevitably will in their humanity, let us fix our eyes on Jesus! Jesus is our ultimate hero and role model. He is our pattern for life and service. He is the "author and perfecter of our faith." He is our Savior and Lord. Choose Him, first and foremost, as your Hero because heroes and role models should be carefully chosen.

I Have Learned That...

The only perfect hero is Jesus Christ! Put Him at the top of your hero list. And keep close tabs on your other role models, making sure they are worthy of the title.

Talking Back

1. Have you ever had any heroes? Is there anyone you really admire or respect who has influenced your life? Who are they?

2. What role can heroes play in our lives – for good or bad?

3. Did Sept. 11, 2001, re-define the word "hero" for you? If so, how?

4. If you had children, whom would you point them to as a hero?

5. In what ways is Jesus the ultimate hero?

Exercising Your Faith

1. Make a list of people who are heroes to you, people you admire or respect. Write them a letter thanking them for their influence in your life.

2. Complete this sentence: I want to be a hero to somebody by ... ."

We Must Seize The Moment While We Have Opportunity

"Carpe diem, lads! Seize the day! Make your lives extraordinary!" These are the words new teacher John Keating speaks to his English literature students at Vermont's exclusive Welton Academy in 1959. The words come to life in the movie, *Dead Poets Society*.

Welton Academy, a private college prep school for boys, is known for grinding out future lawyers, doctors and scientists. The faculty and administration follow a numbing, orthodox, by-the-book approach to education. But one voice stands out among the school's rigid faculty – it belongs to Professor Keating, a Welton alumnus who has returned to the academy to teach English.

Keating uses unorthodox teaching methods and devotes himself to teaching more than just his subject matter, which is poetry. His goal is to inspire his students to "suck the bone of life to the marrow, to seize the day, and make their lives extraordinary."

In Keating's class, you learn lessons about passion, courage and romanticism, as well as poetry. You pass if you avoid conformity and think for yourself. You fail if you neglect to live life to the fullest. Students are challenged to dream and then act on their dreams:

'Tis only in their dreams that men truly be free,
'Twas always thus, and always thus will be. – Keating

Dead Poets Society reminds us to seize and cherish each day dearly. Every day opportunities await us, and we must decide whether to take the chance or merely play it safe.

The Bible also encourages us to seize the moment while we have opportunity: "Be very careful, then, how you live – not as unwise but as wise, making the most of every opportunity, because the days are evil" (Ephesians 5:15-16).

"Whatever your hand finds to do, do it with all your might, for in the grave, where you are going, there is neither working nor planning nor knowledge nor wisdom" (Ecclesiastes 9:10).

Someone once said, "Better to have tried and failed, than to have tried nothing at all and succeeded." How true! We dread the thought of failure, but worse than trying and failing is not trying at all.

Jesus once told a parable about a man who was afraid to seize the moment while he had opportunity. It is a simple story, but it has incredible implications for all of us.

> "Again, it will be like a man going on a journey, who called his servants and entrusted his property to them. To one he gave five talents of money, to another two talents, and to another one talent, each according to his ability. Then he went on his journey. The man who had received the five talents went at once and put his money to work and gained five more. So also, the one with the two talents gained two more. But the man who had received the one talent went off, dug a hole in the ground and hid his master's money.

> After a long time the master of those servants returned and settled accounts with them. The man who had received the five talents brought the other five. 'Master,' he said, 'you entrusted me with five talents. See, I have gained five more.' His master replied, 'Well done, good and faithful servant! You have been faithful with a few things; I will put you in charge of many things. Come and share your master's happiness!'

> The man with the two talents also came. 'Master,' he said, 'you entrusted me with two talents; see, I have gained two more.' His master replied, 'Well done, good and faithful servant! You

have been faithful with a few things; I will put you in charge of many things. Come and share your master's happiness!'

Then the man who had received the one talent came. 'Master,' he said, 'I knew that you are a hard man, harvesting where you have not sown and gathering where you have not scattered seed. So I was afraid and went out and hid your talent in the ground. See, here is what belongs to you.'

His master replied, 'You wicked, lazy servant! So you knew that I harvest where I have not sown and gather where I have not scattered seed? Well then, you should have put my money on deposit with the bankers, so that when I returned I would have received it back with interest.

'Take the talent from him and give it to the one who has the ten talents. For everyone who has will be given more, and he will have an abundance. Whoever does not have, even what he has will be taken from him. And throw that worthless servant outside, into the darkness, where there will be weeping and gnashing of teeth.' " (Matthew 25:14-30)

What did this third servant do that was so wrong? He didn't steal the master's money. He didn't spend it foolishly. He didn't loan it out and lose it. He didn't put it in risky investment and lose it. He kept every penny of it. So, what did he do that was so wrong? *He did nothing.*

He was given an opportunity to do something, and he did nothing. Believe it or not, that is a sin: "Anyone, then, who knows the good he ought to do and doesn't do it, sins" (James 4:17).

What is God's message to us in this parable? Simply this, we must seize the moment while we have opportunity! What were the differences between the "good and faithful servants" and the "wicked and lazy servant?"

Take a Chance or Play It Safe

Successful life involves risk. You have to take chances. In my office are two pictures. One is of an old basketball gymnasium. The caption under the picture reads: "OPPORTUNITY – You'll Always Miss 100

Percent of the Shots You Don't Take."

The other picture is a baseball player sliding safely into second base. The caption reads: "OPPORTUNITY – Opportunity Always Involves Some Risk. You Can't Steal Second Base and Keep Your Foot on First."

In Proverbs 22:13, wise King Solomon put it this way: "The sluggard says, 'There is a lion outside!' or 'I will be murdered in the streets!'"

There will always be lions just outside the door. There will always be excuses for being lazy and not stepping out in faith and taking a chance. The good and faithful servants took chances, while the lazy servant played it safe – and it cost him dearly.

Take Advantage of Opportunities or Make Excuses

When confronted with his lazy inaction, the wicked servant attempted to lay blame at the feet of the master: "Master, I knew that you are a hard man." Notice the good and faithful servants didn't say that – they simply took advantage of the opportunities given them.

We all have certain limitations in life that cannot be changed. I'm 5 feet 9 inches tall and cannot be 6 feet 6 inches tall. That's what I have to work with, and it will not change. We cannot change our parents, our upbringing, or our past mistakes. We cannot change another person without his or her permission. We cannot change the aging process. We cannot eliminate death.

Some people spend their entire lives running away from all the things that challenge them. That's what the lazy servant did. He had less than the other two servants, but he still had enough to do something productive. Instead, he did nothing. I wonder how often that happens to us. The challenge before us is to not make excuses about opportunities we don't have, but take advantage of the opportunities we do have!

Act With Faith or React With Fear

The lazy servant said to his master, "I was afraid and went out and hid your talent in the ground." Fear paralyzes us and keeps us from faith, while faith frees us and keeps us from fear.

In my experience, I have found that there are two primary fears that keep people from seizing the day and taking advantage of their opportunities. We'll call them FOF and FOP.

FOF is fear of failure. "What if I fail?" is the question people afflicted with FOF always ask. Failure is an event, not a person! It is a natural consequence of trying. The only time you really fail at something is when you quit trying. Don't let FOF keep you from seizing the moment.

FOP is fear of people. Some people are so afraid of criticism or ridicule from other people that they never try to fulfill their dreams.

The story is told of an old man whose grandson rode a donkey while they were traveling from one city to another. The man heard some people say, "Would you look at that old man suffering on his feet while that strong young boy is totally capable of walking." So the old man rode the donkey while the boy walked. And he heard people say, "Would you look at that, a healthy man making that poor young boy suffer. Can you believe it?" So the man and the boy both rode the donkey, and they heard some people say, "Would you look at those brutes making that donkey suffer." So they both got off and walked, until they heard some people say, "Would you look at the waste – a perfectly good donkey not being used." Finally, the old man and the grandson both carried the donkey and they never made it to the other city!

No matter what you try to do, people may criticize it. So don't let FOP keep you from seizing the moment.

Act Quickly and Get Results or Procrastinate and Get Nothing

Perhaps the lazy servant was trying to get up the nerve to act, but his master came back before he was ready. Never put off until tomorrow what you could and should do today – seize the moment while you have opportunity!

Leo Buscaglia was a popular professor and author. He often assigned a paper in which his students responded to this question: "If you only had five days to live, how would you spend those five days? And with whom?"

It's a great question to clarify our priorities, isn't it? Students would inevitably give the anticipated answers:

"I'd spend every spare moment with my family and make sure they know how much I love them."

"I'd see all my friends and thank them for their companionship."

"I'd see every sunrise and every sunset."

"I'd write letters and leave them for everyone important in my life."

The students would turn in their papers; and when they got them back, written on them was a note from Dr. Buscaglia:

"Why don't you do these things *now*?"

If you have something you need to be doing, seize the moment! To borrow from the well-known Nike ads, "Just Do It." And do it now, while you have opportunity.

Seize the Moment

Rudy Ruettiger was a young man who had a dream and acted on it, seizing the moment against all odds and in the face of enormous criticism. A movie, simply titled *Rudy,* was made about his seizing the moment experience.

Rudy was one of 14 children growing up in his family in a small town in Illinois. His dream was to attend Notre Dame and play football for the Fighting Irish. But Rudy was only 5 feet 6 inches tall and had graduated third from the bottom in his high school class.

Rudy went into the Navy for a short time and then spent four years working in a power plant. Despite a good job with good benefits, Rudy still wanted to play football for Notre Dame. Of course, it was a one-in-a-million goal, and his family and friends repeatedly told him so, but he quit his job and moved to South Bend, Ind.

Obstacle after obstacle was in his path, but Rudy was determined at least to give his best effort. He was refused admission to Notre Dame because of his poor high school transcript. The admissions counselor told him if he attended nearby Holy Cross Junior College and made straight A's four semesters in a row, he would be admitted to Notre Dame. Although he had never made better than a C in high school and was discovered to be dyslexic, he made the necessary grades!

But, of course, being a student at Notre Dame and being on the Irish football team are very different. At 5 feet 6 inches tall and 190 pounds, Rudy just wanted to make the practice team, even if he never dressed out for a game. The coaches discouraged him from trying out for the squad and told him he would never play in a game, but Rudy wouldn't give up his dream.

For two years, Rudy worked out with one of the greatest teams in college football history, serving mostly as a punching bag for the bigger, faster, more talented varsity players. On Saturday, he watched the game from the stands, like any other fan.

In the last home game of his senior year, Rudy was allowed to dress out at the request of several varsity players. His hard work, enthusiasm and never-give-up spirit caused him to be something of a hero among the players, students and fans. Near the end of the game, with Notre Dame leading, the players and fans began chanting, "Rudy! Rudy! Rudy!"

Coach Dan Devine sent Rudy into the game with 27 seconds left to play. On the last play of the game, Rudy sacked the Georgia Tech quarterback. The Irish players lifted Rudy to their shoulders and carried him off the field. In the history of Notre Dame football, no player has been carried off the field on the shoulders of other players – except Rudy!

Rudy's dream didn't end with a 27-second college football career. He sold Hollywood his story, and he now makes a healthy income writing and speaking to sales organizations and youth groups.

Rudy Ruettiger is an excellent example of what can happen when a motivated young person seizes the moment and seeks to make his or her life extraordinary.

I Have Learned That...

Just as the master in Jesus' parable gave his servants money to manage for him, God has given you a life to manage for Him. He has given you talents and opportunities. Don't waste them. Seize the moment while you have opportunity!

Talking Back

1. In Jesus' parable, what did the third servant do that was so wrong? How does that apply to us?

2. Why do you think people avoid taking advantage of opportunities? Discuss the phrase, "You can't steal second base and keep your foot on first."

3. Are you more tempted by fear of failure or fear of people? How can we overcome our FOF and FOP?

4. What spiritual opportunities have you put off until later? Why have you procrastinated?

5. Is there something you could do right now to seize the moment and make your life extraordinary?

Exercising Your Faith

1. Take Leo Buscaglia's challenge: Write a short essay on the topic, "If I only had five days to live, how would I spend those five days? And with whom?" And then, challenge yourself to do those things *now*!

2. Rent and watch the movie *Rudy*, and let it inspire your heart to follow your dreams and try to make your life extraordinary.

Money Can Be A Blessing or a Curse

A man in southern California was on his way to work one morning in his new BMW when the "big one" hit. The earth began to tremble under his wheels, and his car was swallowed by the earth. As the seriously injured man climbed out of the wreckage he didn't notice that his left arm had been cut off at the elbow. He stood by the side of the road, viewing the wreckage and crying out, "Oh no, my Beemer, my Beemer!"

"How can you be crying about your car?" asked a man who had witnessed the disaster. "Don't you realize that your arm has been cut off?"

The man looked down in horror at his missing arm and said, "Oh, no! My Rolex! My Rolex!"

This man represents the materialistic society in which we live – a culture where money is the driving force behind much of what happens in our daily lives. A recent Gallup poll of families in America asked the question, "What is the biggest problem you face as a family?" Fifty-six percent of the families responded that money and economic problems were the biggest problem they face. The next highest category was health problems and health care at only 6 percent!

The magazine, *Psychology Today*, published an article titled, "The One Who Has the Most Toys When He Dies, Wins." The article quoted a survey that has been conducted every year since 1966 of college freshmen. In the 30 years between 1966 and 1996 the answers changed dramatically. In 1966 more than 80 percent of college freshmen said that the major reason for attending college was "to develop a meaningful philosophy of life." In 1996, 70 percent of college freshmen said that the major reason for attending college was to be able to make more money.

Money is probably the number one master in American life today. And yet more people are unhappy and discontented than ever before. America is full of people who wear shackles of gold, live in carpeted prisons, and are bound with ropes of silk. They are just as enslaved by the love of money as poor people are by the lack of money.

Money makes a great servant but a terrible master. Money can be a blessing or a curse. It all depends on whether you handle it or it handles you!

Misconceptions About Money

This may surprise you but the Bible has much to say about money matters, because money matters. More than 2,000 verses in the Bible are about money, possessions and finances. Let's look at some misconceptions about money – beliefs that are not true, but they often determine how people handle their possessions.

■ *"God is anti-wealth."* Contrary to what you may have heard, God is not upset when you work hard and earn a large amount of money. The Bible is not anti-wealth, anti-capitalism or anti-ownership. In fact, throughout the Bible we are encouraged to work hard, be diligent, support our families, do our best, and be generous with others.

Some of the wealthiest men of Scripture were also some of the godliest men of Scripture: Abraham, David, Job and Solomon are just a few examples. God did not punish these men for their wealth; He loved them and blessed them.

■ *"Money is the root of all evil."* Some people think this phrase is in the Bible, but there is one key word left out of the actual Bible verse: "For the LOVE of money is a root of all kinds of evil. Some people, eager for money, have wandered from the faith and pierced themselves with many griefs" (1 Timothy 6:10).

See the difference? Money is not evil; it is neutral. The inordinate love of money which causes people to wander from the faith and make money their master is evil.

■ *"If I have enough money, I will be happy."* We all have known poor people who were happy and rich people who were miserable. Money simply doesn't buy happiness. Even if it did, the happiness would be temporary: "Do not wear yourself out to get rich; have the wisdom to show restraint. Cast but a glance at riches, and they are gone, for they will surely sprout wings and fly off to the sky like an eagle" (Proverbs 23:4-5).

■ *"If I had enough money, I would feel secure."* Actually, money may produce a false sense of security:

> Now listen, you who say, "Today or tomorrow we will go to this or that city, spend a year there, carry on business and make money." Why, you do not even know what will happen tomorrow. What is your life? You are a mist that appears for a little while and then vanishes (James 4:13-14).

People with great wealth are tempted to feel invincible and in control of everything in their lives. Jesus told a story about a man with this attitude:

> "The ground of a certain rich man produced a good crop. He thought to himself, 'What shall I do? I have no place to store my crops.'
>
> "Then he said, 'This is what I'll do. I will tear down my barns and build bigger ones, and there I will store all my grain and my goods. And I'll say to myself, "You have plenty of good things laid up for many years. Take life easy; eat, drink, and be merry."'
>
> "But God said to him, 'You fool! This very night your life will be demanded from you. Then who will get what you have prepared for yourself?"
>
> "This is how it will be with anyone who stores up things for himself but is not rich toward God" (Luke 12:16-21).

This man's downfall was believing if he had enough money and good things stored up, he would be secure and safe. And that is basically the belief system of the materialistic culture around us at the dawn of the 21st century. Actually, Jesus prefaced this parable with a verse as appropriate for our times as it was when spoken nearly 2,000 years ago:

"Watch out! Be on your guard against all kinds of greed; a man's life does not consist in the abundance of his possessions" (Luke 12:15), which leads us to the next major misconception.

■ *"My wealth determines my worth."* This may be the biggest misconception of all. Jesus clearly said that one's life, one's worth, is not determined by one's wealth. The poorest person in the world is not the person who has no money, but the person who has nothing but money.

Someone once said, "Measure wealth not by the things you have, but by the things you have for which you would not take money." Always remember that what you are is far more important than what you have. "Better a poor man whose walk is blameless than a rich man whose ways are perverse" (Proverbs 28:6).

How Money Can Be A Curse

Because money can be a blessing or a curse, we must be careful how we use it. Here are some ways money can be a curse.

■ *Money can be a curse when you have too much debt.* Seniors in high school and freshmen in college begin receiving all kinds of enticing credit card applications in the mail. Creditors are attempting to hook you early and begin a pattern of debt that can be destructive all your life. Avoid credit card debt because you will be a big loser! "The rich rule over the poor, and the borrower is servant to the lender" (Proverbs 22:7).

Signing the back of a credit card is a binding agreement. The credit company agrees to loan you money to buy things, and you agree to pay them the amount you borrow (plus any fees or interest, and the interest is often between 15-25 percent). Credit cards are not secured by property, which means you can spend money you don't have and pile up tons of debt.

Credit companies make their money by charging interest when you don't pay the full bill. Often you can wind up paying more than double the cost of your purchases through interest. Debt is the opposite of savings. You either earn interest through savings or you pay interest through debt. Savings earn; debt costs. Isn't it obvious which is better?

■ *Money can be a curse when we trust it more than God.* Listen to the words of a wise man named Agur in Proverbs 30:7-9:

> Two things I ask of you, O Lord; do not refuse me before I die: Keep falsehood and lies far from me; give me neither poverty nor riches, but give me only my daily bread. Otherwise, I may have too much and disown you and say, "Who is the Lord?" Or I may become poor and steal, and so dishonor the name of my God.

I cannot tell you how many times I have witnessed Agur's words become prophetic in the lives of people I've known. Too much prosperity changed their values and slowly eroded their commitment to the Lord. When we become more interested in the gold standard than the God standard we are headed for spiritual trouble.

A man who was very close to me was raised in a Christian family and attended a Christian school. In his late teens he did some preaching and considered going into ministry. His values and standards were strong and unquestioned. Then he had some early success in business and made a considerable fortune. He slowly began to pull away from God and the church. Now, several years later, he claims to be an agnostic with zero interest in God or the church. Everyone who knows him agrees on the cause: Give me not riches. "Otherwise I may have too much and disown you and say, 'Who is the Lord?' "

■ *Money can be a curse when it becomes the most important priority in your life.* People who make decisions based solely on money often find these decisions come back to haunt them. Jesus told of such a young man:

> As Jesus started on his way, a man ran up to him and fell on his knees before him. "Good teacher," he asked, "what must I do to inherit eternal life?"

> "Why do you call me good?" Jesus answered. "No one is good – except God alone. You know the commandments: 'Do not murder, do not commit adultery, do not steal, do not give false testimony, do not defraud, honor your father and mother.'"

> "Teacher," he declared, "all these I have kept since I was a boy."

Jesus looked at him and loved him. "One thing you lack," he said. "Go, sell everything you have and give to the poor, and you will have treasure in heaven. Then come, follow me."

At this the man's face fell. He went away sad, because he had great wealth (Mark 10:17-22).

This young man's problem was the "one thing" most important in his life – money – even more important than eternal life!

How Money Can Be a Blessing

Enough of the negative! Let's look at some ways money can be a blessing.

■ *Money can be a blessing when you enjoy and are thankful for the material blessings God has given you.* There will always be people who have more money than you … and there will always be people who have less money than you. Too many people are not thankful to God for what they have because they are so focused on what they don't have. God wants us to enter his "gates with thanksgiving and his courts with praise; give thanks to him and praise his name" (Psalm 100:4).

■ *Money can be a blessing when you save it.* You don't have to spend everything you have, and you most certainly don't need to spend what you don't have by going into debt and paying interest! Plan ahead about spending and saving your money: "The plans of the diligent lead to profit as surely as haste leads to poverty" (Proverbs 21:5).

Saving even a small amount on a regular basis can accumulate into a significant amount of money: "[H]e who gathers money little by little makes it grow" (Proverbs 13:11). "The wise man saves for the future, but the foolish man spends whatever he gets" (21:20 TLB).

You either earn interest through savings or you pay interest through debt. The only way ever to get ahead financially is to earn interest, not pay it!

■ *Money can be a blessing when you give it.* Nobody is ever really remembered for what they got out of life, but what they gave to life. Both the Old and New Testaments teach this important truth:

> Honor the Lord with your wealth, with the firstfruits of all your crops; then your barns will be filled to overflowing, and your vats will brim over with new wine (Proverbs 3:9-10).

> A generous man will himself be blessed, for he shares his food with the poor (Proverbs 22:9).

> "Give, and it will be given to you. A good measure, pressed down, shaken together and running over, will be poured into your lap. For with the measure you use, it will be measured to you" (Luke 6:38).

Jesus said, "It is more blessed to give than to receive" (Acts 20:35). Jesus then practiced what He preached by giving His own life up for us!

I've learned that these Scriptures are true – you simply cannot out-give God! God says that when you obey Him in giving to Him and to others in need that He takes care of you. In other words, your investment brings God's involvement.

There is nothing wrong with having things money can buy, as long as you don't lose the things that money can't buy. Enough money can buy anything that is for sale, but the most important things in life – love, lasting satisfaction, a loyal relationship with God – are not for sale.

A true story from the life of our nation's 28th president, Woodrow Wilson, illustrates this point. President Wilson was campaigning on a train, crossing the country from town to town. He stopped in Billings, Mont., to speak to a crowd from the back of the train. A little boy got close enough to the president to hand him something wrapped in a piece of paper. It was not at all uncommon for people to give the president gifts.

Five years later when Woodrow Wilson died in office, they discovered in his billfold what that little boy had given him wrapped in that piece of paper – a dime. That's all, just a dime.

Why had the president kept that dime for five years in his billfold? It certainly wasn't the amount that had value to him – he kept it because that dime represented love that a little boy was expressing for his president. You see, it's not the amount of the gift but the heart of the giver that really matters.

I Have Learned That...

Missionary Jim Eliot once said, "He is no fool who gives up what he cannot keep in order to gain that which he cannot lose." Don't be like the rich young ruler, holding on to what you cannot keep anyway (money, material things) and missing out on eternal life. Make money your servant, not your master because money can be a blessing or a curse – it depends on whether you handle it or it handles you!

Talking Back

1. Discuss the phrase, "Money makes a great servant, but it makes a terrible master." How can money enslave people?

2. Read 1 Timothy 6:10. How is the "love of money a root of all kinds of evil"?

3. If it is obvious that saving is better than debt, why are so many people enslaved to debt? What do you understand about debt, interest and savings?

4. What are some ways we can share our material blessings with others?

5. Jesus said, "It is more blessed to give than to receive." What does that mean to you?

Exercising Your Faith

1. Take a personal field trip to a bank. Open a savings account and every time you receive money, put a small portion of it in your savings account to earn interest.

2. Determine to give back to God. Support an orphan or underprivileged child or perhaps a missionary. Ask your elders, minister or youth minister where you could best give a few dollars each month to help a good cause.

We Can Either Seethe in Anger Or Soothe in Peace

A boy once asked his father, "Dad, how do wars begin?" The father replied, "Well, son, take World War I, for example. It all started when Germany invaded Belgium."

Immediately, his wife interrupted, "That's not how it happened. It began when that archduke was murdered."

The husband scowled and snapped back, "Are you answering the question or am I?"

Turning with a huff, the wife stormed out of the room, slamming the door on the way out. An uneasy silence followed.

After a moment the silence was broken by the boy who said, "Dad, you don't have to tell me anymore. I know now."

Indeed, anger and angry outbursts start wars – wars between countries and wars between people. Relationships are damaged or destroyed by uncontrolled anger. A verse in an old hymn, "Angry Words," describes the harmful effect of anger on our relationships:

> Angry words are lightly spoken,
> Bitt'rest tho'ts are rashly stirred,
> Brightest links of life are broken
> By a single angry word.

We have a choice about anger – we can either seethe in anger or we can soothe in peace. Soothing is much better than seething! Let's look at three important questions about soothing and seething.

Why Do People Get Angry?

Why do you get angry? What really makes you mad? If you are like most people, I think your answers will fall into one of three categories:

■ *Violated convictions and/or perceived injustice.* Every person develops beliefs about how people should act and how things should be done. When people behave in ways that violate our convictions, or do things we consider to be an injustice, we get angry.

On Sept. 11, 2001, our nation was appalled and grieved when terrorists attacked our country and killed thousands of innocent victims. We angrily wondered, "How could this happen? And why do the terrorists hate us that much?"

But, it's not just foreign terrorists who act in evil and unjust ways. In 1995, the Murrah Federal Building in Oklahoma City was similarly attacked with a bomb, killing hundreds of innocent people. The perpetrator was an American man, angry at our government.

In the Bible, Moses was so angry by Israel's idolatry in making a golden calf that he threw down the Ten Commandments tablets, shattering them (Exodus 32:19). And God became so angry with the Israelites that He made them wander in the desert for 40 years (Numbers 32:13).

Responding in anger – over murder, evil and injustice – comes from the violations of convictions about right and wrong and concern for injustice. Such anger is not sin if it is properly channeled to a desire to defend God's laws and protect others from harm. It can become sin if it degenerates into anger merely over how an injustice inconveniences us personally or leads to self-centered revenge: "Do not take revenge, my friends, but leave room for God's wrath, for it is written: 'It is mine to avenge; I will repay,' says the Lord" (Romans 12:19).

■ *Personal pain.* When our sense of personal safety is threatened, we experience hurt and fear. We often hide those feelings with an emotional response of anger. Children of divorce often experience this kind of anger. Deeply hurt by the breakup of their family and the perceived rejection of one or both parents, they lash out in anger.

Many of the perpetrators of school shootings in America were expressing their hostility toward others in response to the personal pain of rejection, disrespect or loneliness. Although the hurt may be legitimate, the angry retaliation is not. There is a better way to handle personal pain, as we will notice later.

■ *Our goals are not being met, or our needs or desires are being blocked.* James 4:1-3 reads:

> What causes fights and quarrels among you? Don't they come from your desires that battle within you? You want something but you don't get it. You kill and covet, but you cannot have what you want. You quarrel and fight. You do not have, because you do not ask God. When you ask, you do not receive, because you ask with wrong motives, that you may spend what you get on your pleasures.

The Bible clearly says that a major source of our anger is desiring something and not getting it. So we quarrel and fight and angrily demand our way. Obviously, this is a sinful kind of anger.

Is Anger Always Sinful?

Ephesians 4:26-27 reads, "In your anger do not sin: Do not let the sun go down while you are still angry, and do not give the devil a foothold."

These verses reveal three important truths about anger:

1. *Anger is not always sin.* Clearly, the Bible teaches there is an anger that is not sinful.
2. *Anger should have a time limitation.* Sinless anger should not linger past sundown, or into the next day. Anger becomes sin when we allow it to linger.
3. *Anger that lingers gives the devil a foothold in our lives.* The devil is always looking for our vulnerable spot, and he can use lingering anger to create pain in our lives and in our relationships with others.

We know anger, in and of itself, is not sinful because Jesus was angry and He was sinless. His righteous anger caused Him to drive the greedy and corrupt money changers from the temple (John 2:13-17). God was often angry with the Israelites because of their disobedience: "The Lord's anger burned against Israel and he made them wander in the desert forty years, until the whole generation of those who had done evil in his sight was gone" (Numbers 32:13). Clearly, we can see that not all anger is sinful. There are some major differences between righteous and unrighteous, sinful anger.

Righteous Anger	*Unrighteous Anger*
• Controlled, with purpose	• Uncontrolled rage, without purpose or patience
• No hatred, rage or resentment	• With hatred, rage or resentment
• Unselfish	• Selfish
• To correct destructive behavior	• To destroy the person
• As an expression of care and correction	• As an expression of revenge
• At injustice	• At violations of self

If all anger is not sin, when is anger sinful?

■ *When it is directed toward the person, not the problem.* We may be angry at sin (as was the Lord), but we are to love the sinner (as did the Lord). Focus righteous anger on the problem, not the person!

■ *When it leads you to revenge or vengeanc*e. "Do not take revenge, my friends, but leave room for God's wrath, for it is written: 'It is mine to avenge; I will repay,' says the Lord" (Romans 12:19).

If you are so angry at someone that you either silently or openly have made up your mind not to forgive that person, or at least not to forgive that person until you have hurt them or evened the score, then your anger is sinful.

■ *When you hold on to it and allow it to become a way of life.* Any number of scriptures are instructive at this point:

A hot-tempered man stirs up dissension, but a patient man calms a quarrel (Proverbs 15:18).

> Do not make friends with a hot-tempered man, do not associate with one easily angered, or you may learn his ways and get yourself ensnared (Proverbs 22:24-25).

> Like a city whose walls are broken down is a man who lacks self-control (Proverbs 25:28).

> A fool gives full vent to his anger, but a wise man keeps himself under control (Proverbs 29:11).

Don't hold on to anger. Get rid of it quickly and appropriately so that you do not give the devil a foothold in your life!

■ *When it acts in wrong ways.* Ephesians 4:30 tells us not to "grieve the Holy Spirit of God," and in the next verse tells us how we grieve Him: "Get rid of all bitterness, rage and anger, brawling and slander, along with every form of malice" (v. 31). This verse gives us the chain reaction of the explosion of a lost temper:

- *Bitterness.* This is the "somebody done me wrong" song. Anger begins when the seed of bitterness is planted in the soil of your heart. If that bitterness is not rooted up and then rooted out, it will turn into sinful anger.
- *Rage.* The Greek word for rage literally means "to burn." Have you ever seen a fire raging out of control, consuming everything in its path? That's what sinful anger does to a person – it burns in their heart, ready for any type of fuel to fan it into a raging, uncontrolled fire.
- *Brawling and slander.* The word brawling literally means "loud quarreling." Have you ever noticed that the angrier you get, the more you tend to raise your voice? Have you ever been in an argument with someone and they say to you, "You don't have to yell." And you yell back, "I'M NOT YELLING!"
- *Every form of malice.* This word literally means wickedness or evil. This is when the inward attitudes and thoughts turn into outward actions.

We see this chain reaction of anger throughout our society. Teen killers go on shooting sprees in schools and people wonder, "Why?" Because bitterness translates into rage and then evil actions. Terrorists attack America and people wonder, "Why?" Because years of anger turn into bitterness, then rage, then evil actions. When a person's temper gets the best of him, it reveals the worst of him!

How Can We Soothe Instead of Seethe?

Now don't cop out and say, "I just can't control my temper." That is simply not true! You control your temper when it is in your best interest. Have you ever been in an argument with someone in your family with everyone yelling and venting? About that time the phone rings and someone picks it up and calmly says, "Hello." Anger can be controlled and temper can be tamed anytime we choose to do so. In other words, you can choose to soothe instead of seethe! How?

■ *Commit to an attitude of peace rather than pain.* The best place to start is with the teaching of Jesus:

> "You have heard that it was said, 'Eye for eye, and tooth for tooth.' But I tell you, Do not resist an evil person. If someone strikes you on the right cheek, turn to him the other also" (Matthew 5:38-39).

This teaching is often misunderstood. Jesus is not giving a legalistic formula for how to respond to angry people. He is contrasting how things generally work in the world with what life looks like in the kingdom of God. Jesus is saying here that we must make a basic decision: Our commitment to act in love is not contingent on the behavior of other people.

This does not mean that we let people abuse us. A loving response to anger might well involve confrontation and difficult words. Jesus' point is not that we are never to do anything that might cause an angry person pain. He is simply saying that Christians are to be different from a world that automatically says, "You hurt me, and I'll hurt you back." This begins with a basic commitment to an attitude of seeking peace rather than pain.

■ *Confront anger when you feel it coming on.* When you feel anger rising up within you, remind yourself of what God says about a quick temper:

> A quick-tempered man does foolish things (Proverbs 14:17).

A hot-tempered man stirs up dissension, but a patient man calms a quarrel (Proverbs 15:18).

When someone makes us angry, we have a tendency to let him know about it right away. You may have already learned this doesn't work. You blow off some steam and might feel a little better for the moment, but you often cause more damage than you can repair. And, more often than not, you end up looking foolish.

Before you blow up in anger, give yourself time to think things over.

A fool shows his annoyance at once, but a prudent man overlooks an insult (Proverbs 12:16).

Someone once advised, "When you are angry, count to 10 before you speak. If you are real angry, count to 100 and then don't say anything." That is good advice. I think the Lord agrees with this advice because James 1:19-20 reads, "My dear brothers, take note of this: Everyone should be quick to listen, slow to speak, and slow to become angry, for man's anger does not bring about the righteous life that God desires." Confront your anger when you feel it rising up within you.

■ *Confine your anger to specific limitations.* We have already noticed one important limitation: "Do not let the sun go down while you are still angry, and do not give the devil a foothold" (Ephesians 4:26-27). Don't go to bed angry. Don't carry your anger into a new day. Deal with your anger before it grows – it will never be easier to control than at the beginning. In old Western movies and TV shows, the sheriff would often say to the bad guy, "I want you out of town by sundown." If you want to control your temper, you will have to stare down your angry feelings and say, "I want you gone, out of my life, by sundown." That's biblical and wise!

Also, in confining your anger, you can choose to de-escalate it. Proverbs gives us still more counsel on making this wise choice:

A gentle answer turns away wrath, but a harsh word stirs up anger (Proverbs 15:1).

Through patience a ruler can be persuaded, and a gentle tongue can break a bone (Proverbs 25:15).

Ironically, the more you give into the temptation to defend yourself when angrily attacked, the more it feeds your attacker's desire to attack you! Choosing to de-escalate such anger with a gentle answer will turn away wrath.

■ *Confess your anger to God, and perhaps to others.* If you feel yourself getting angry, don't try to excuse it or hold it in, confess it to the Lord. Just pray, "Lord, I am getting angry. Help me not sin in my anger. Help me get rid of those angry feelings quickly and properly." Pray a prayer of confession over and over again until you feel the anger begin to subside.

Let me illustrate what often happens with anger. Fill a glass of water to the halfway point. Then slowly pour in more water until the glass is filled to the top. Then pour a few more drops in the glass that is full to the brim. Of course, it spills over the top and out of the glass. The point is simple – when a glass is already full, it only takes a few drops to spill.

That happens to people, too. When a person keeps exploding in anger, it is usually because his or her glass is already full of pain. Unresolved pain usually turns to anger. If you find yourself often angry, check the levels in your "emotional glass." Perhaps the hurts of rejection, or abuse, or betrayal, or divorce, or neglect, etc., have filled your glass to the point that even small frustrations spill over into angry outbursts.

What do you do about your full glass? You confess to God your problems and trust Him to help care for you: "Cast all your anxiety on him because he cares for you" (1 Peter 5:7).

It may also help to confess your anger to another person who can empathize with you and hold you accountable. After all, James 5:16 says, "[C]onfess your sins to each other and pray for each other so that you may be healed. The prayer of a righteous man is powerful and effective."

Tell someone who loves you, someone you can trust, someone who will hold you accountable before God. Sometimes another person, with a calm spirit and an objective mind, can help you avoid angry outbursts that turn into terrible tragedies.

I Have Learned That...

You don't have to live in a war zone of anger. You can choose peace over pain, and you should, for I've learned that soothing is far better than seething!

Talking Back

1. Why do you get angry? What really makes you angry?

2. Is anger always sinful? If not, when is anger appropriate?

3. Read the various Proverbs in this chapter. Which one do you like best and why?

4. What specifically can people do to seek peace rather than pain?

5. Ephesians 4:26-27 suggests some specific limitations to put on anger. What are they? What limitations could you add that would help control and confine anger?

Exercising Your Faith

1. When you feel angry, start keeping an "anger journal." Write down your reasons for being angry and write down whether or not it is sinful or appropriate anger. Pray about it before the sun goes down.

2. Look for someone who is experiencing anger. Reach out to that person with the love of God – through a note, a smile, a conversation, a prayer, etc.

Friends Can Make You or Break You

I saw a cartoon once, and the first frame showed a masked thief pointing his gun toward a frightened victim. In the next scene the robber is holding out a sack and saying, "Give me all your valuables!" The final scene shows the victim stuffing into the sack all of his friends.

This man knew his real "valuables" were his friends. Why are friends so valuable?

Characteristics of a True Friend

Friends are essential because they meet many needs in our lives. Consider these characteristics of a true friend who meets our needs.

■ *A true friend hurts when you hurt.* Think of the people you call your best friends. When you hurt, do they hurt? Or do they secretly rejoice? If it's the latter, they're not really your friends.

I once read a definition of a true friend as "someone who will walk into your house when the whole world has just walked out." In other words, they hurt when you hurt.

In the Old Testament, Job was a man who was hurting because he had lost his family, his wealth, and his health. His "friends" implied that his problems were his own fault, the result of his sin. So Job said, "A despairing man should have the devotion of his friends. … But my brothers are as undependable as intermittent streams" (Job 6:14-15). Job was right – when we are hurting and in despair, we will have the devotion of a true friend.

■ *A true friend rejoices when you rejoice.* The Bible teaches that a characteristic of sincere love is to "[r]ejoice with those who rejoice" (Romans 12:9, 15). A true friend is not threatened by your achievements or jealous of your successes, but rejoices with you in your accomplishments. Someone once wrote, "A true friend is one who multiplies your joys and divides your grief."

■ *A true friend is loyal to your friendship.* Proverbs 18:24 reads, "A man of many companions may come to ruin, but there is a friend who sticks closer than a brother." The word "stick" refers to how the skin sticks to the bone. Here is a picture of how a real friend will stick closer to you than your skin will stick to your own bone.

If you want to find out who your friends really are, it is easy to determine – just make a mistake and see how they react. A true friend will still be loyal to your friendship.

■ *A true friend will tell you the truth in love.* A true friend will say to you what needs to be said, when it needs to be said, even if it hurts a little bit. With a true friend, both of you know that the words are not intended to hurt but to help. Solomon wrote, "Wounds from a friend can be trusted, but an enemy multiplies kisses" (Proverbs 27:6).

Truth and love are not always joined together. We are to speak the truth – that's honesty and integrity – but we are to speak the truth in love, not with jealousy, arrogance, anger or self-righteousness (Ephesians 4:15).

Our human nature is that we often go to one extreme or the other. By nature, we usually are very sentimental and non-confrontational and speak mostly love; or we are very stern and practical and speak mostly truth. If you have a true friend who is able to find the proper balance of telling you the truth in love, you have a very valuable gift!

■ *A true friend will seek to bring out the best in you.* When you bring a friend into your inner circle, you can be sure they will have an influence on your life. So, seek out friends who can bring out the best in you. "As iron sharpens iron, so one man sharpens another" (Proverbs 27:17).

Choose friends with characteristics you admire and characteristics you want to see in your own life. Chances are good their character will ultimately rub off on you. "He who walks with the wise grows wise, but a companion of fools suffers harm" (Proverbs 13:20).

■ *A true friend shares unconditional love with you.* On one occasion when my family moved from one town to another, a good friend we were leaving behind gave us a beautiful cross-stitched quote: "A true friend is one who knows all about you and loves you just the same."

Some people are your friends conditionally, as long as it is convenient for them. I heard about a little boy who walked into the dentist's office with a friend of his, and said, "Doc, I've got a tooth that's got to come out right now, and I don't want any gas; I don't want any novocaine; I don't want any shots to deaden the pain. My friend and I have a lot of things we want to do today, and we want to hurry and get this tooth out right now."

The doctor was very impressed and said, "Son, I have never seen a young man with courage like yours. Which tooth is it?"

The little boy turned to his friend and said, "Show him your tooth, Tommy."

In a true friendship, your friend will want what is best for you, not what is best for himself.

Friends Can Also Break You

One of the saddest stories in the Bible is the story of Amnon, the son of King David, who tricked and raped his half-sister and was eventually murdered by his brother. It is a story that literally screams out at us to be very careful in choosing our friends because we may, at the same time, be choosing our fate:

> In the course of time, Amnon son of David fell in love with Tamar, the beautiful sister of Absalom son of David. Amnon became frustrated to the point of illness on account of his sister Tamar, for she was a virgin, and it seemed impossible for him to do anything to her (2 Samuel 13:1-2).

Amnon said he loved his half-sister so much that he was sick with love for her. But Amnon at least had some sense of right and wrong, some sense of conscience, because he had not done anything wrong and "it seemed impossible for him to do anything to her." But watch the next line: "Now Amnon had a friend named Jonadab son of Shimeah, David's brother. Jonadab was a very shrewd man" (2 Samuel 13:3).

Jonadab laid out a wicked plot for Amnon, telling him exactly how to sin and encouraging him to do wrong:

> "Go to bed and pretend to be ill," Jonadab said. "When your father comes to see you, say to him, 'I would like my sister Tamar to come and give me something to eat. Let her prepare the food in my sight so I may watch her and then eat it from her hand'" (2 Samuel 13:5).

Amnon carried through on the evil plot his friend Jonadab had schemed and raped his half-sister (2 Samuel 13:6-14). This set off a chain reaction of events in Amnon's family that ended with his own murder by his vengeful half-brother Absalom, Tamar's full brother (vv. 23-29).

It is a sad and sordid story. Amnon had no defense – he was guilty as sin. He made his own choice, but his choice was plotted by his so-called friend. This is why the Bible teaches: "Do not be misled: 'Bad company corrupts good character'" (1 Corinthians 15:33).

There is another lesson here that needs to be addressed. Although Amnon said he loved Tamar, his attraction to her was not love, but lust! You say, "How do you know that?" Look at 2 Samuel 13:15: "Then Amnon hated her with intense hatred. In fact, he hated her more than he had loved her. Amnon said to her, 'Get up and get out!'"

As soon as he had gratified his lust, his love turned to hate. True love does not turn on and off like that, and true love waits for marriage to initiate an intimate sexual relationship.

Make-or-Break Friendships

Because you will have friends, let me share a few practical points for you to consider.

■ *Your friends can be your greatest asset or your greatest liability.* If I had a dollar for every time somebody has sat across from me in counseling and said, "My friends got me in trouble," I would be a rich man! But it's often a true statement – even Amnon could have said it.

If you visited the jail in your city today, you would be amazed how many of the inmates would say they are there because they had the wrong kind of friends. Some friend taught them how to commit a crime, how to steal, how to buy and/or sell drugs.

Actor Don Johnson became a big star doing the *Miami Vice* TV series in the late '80s and early '90s. When his acting career started in the '70s, he got caught up in the Hollywood lifestyle and spent a decade taking drugs, abusing alcohol, and "living it up." In the mid-'80s he finally got his personal life straightened out and got sober. He was once asked if he had any regrets. He said, "Yes, I regret wasting lots of time with a bunch of jerks that I wish I hadn't spent 10 minutes with now, let alone 10 years!"

By the way, the influence of friends cuts both ways. It can be good as well as bad. I thank God regularly that I came under the influence of friends who helped me grow in my love for the Lord.

Who are you running around with and why? Who are you buddying up to? What kind of friends do you have, and what kind of friends are you seeking out? I can tell you from personal experience, from counseling experience, and from the Word of God that your friends can be your greatest asset or your greatest liability.

■ *You are or will become like your friends.* Most of us either are what our friends are or we soon will be. If that is not tue, then why are they our friends?

The old saying, "Birds of a feather flock together," is true. Ducks run with ducks because they are ducks. They don't run with cows. And cows hang out with other cows because they are cows. They don't associate with chickens. Do you know why chickens run around with other chickens? Because they are chickens.

Generally speaking, people hang out with people who have similar interests, goals and values. And they slowly influence one another until they become like one another. Doesn't it make sense then for Christian teens to hang out with other Christian teens?

During the teen years, the influence of friends can often be stronger than the influence of parents. Amnon is a good example of peer influence. I do not suppose there is a young man in all the world – past, present or future – who could ever say any more proudly than Amnon could have said, "David is my dad."

Think about it. David is the only man in the Bible about whom God ever said he is a man after His own heart. That was Amnon's dad.

David wrote more than half the Psalms, including the beautiful 23rd Psalm. He was the mighty king of Israel. He was a champion warrior from his youth, having saved Israel by killing Goliath. From David's family tree came Jesus Christ. You talk about a great family, Amnon had one; but his friend Jonadab's influence was greater than his father's influence.

Be careful choosing your friends because chances are you will become like them!

■ *You are known by the friends you keep.* Because of my position as a minister, I have had several occasions in which people were scrambling for explanations about the friends I saw them with. The funny thing is, I probably didn't think anything about it, but their guilty conscience demanded they give an explanation.

Christians must be careful about making friends because there is a guilt-by-association reality in friendship. Like it or not, you are known by the friends you keep.

Second Corinthians 6:14-15 warns Christians about close associations with unbelievers:

> Do not be yoked together with unbelievers. For what do righteousness and wickedness have in common? Or what fellowship can light have with darkness? What harmony is there between Christ and Belial? What does a believer have in common with an unbeliever?

I don't think the Bible is teaching that we shouldn't have any friends who are unbelievers, and I'm not suggesting that either. If that were true, how would we ever convert someone to Christ? But I am suggesting that:

- We should influence them for good, not allowing them to influence us for bad; and
- We should also be constantly developing close Christian friendships that will encourage and strengthen us.

The inescapable reality is you will be known by the friends you keep.

■ *Your future is often dependent upon your friends.* Amnon forfeited his future because he did what his friend suggested. Take a quick look at Amnon's future: Tamar told her brother Absalom what Amnon had done. Absalom told her to keep it quiet, and he took her to his house to live with him. Absalom "hated Amnon because he had disgraced his sister Tamar" (2 Samuel 13:22). Two years passed and Absalom exacted his revenge:

> Absalom ordered his men, "Listen! When Amnon is in high spirits from drinking wine and I say to you, 'Strike Amnon down,' then kill him. Don't be afraid. Have I not given you this order? Be strong and brave." So Absalom's men did to Amnon what Absalom had ordered (2 Samuel 13:28-29).

Notice, by the way, that Jonadab is nowhere to be found when the punishment comes down. The friends like Jonadab will never be there to take even partial responsibility for leading someone astray!

In fact, this is incredible, but apparently Jonadab knew that Absalom was going to kill Amnon. He told King David, "My lord should not think that they killed all the princes; only Amnon is dead. This has been Absalom's expressed intention ever since the day Amnon raped his sister Tamar" (2 Samuel 13:32).

What a friend! Not only did Jonadab not tell David that he had helped plot the crime, but apparently he also knew of Absalom's intention to kill Amnon, and he didn't tell his friend! With friends like that, who needs enemies?

Amnon was royalty, the son of a king, in line potentially to succeed his father as King of Israel, but he was dead and had forfeited his future because of the wicked advice and influence of a friend. It can happen to any of us.

A Modern-Day Amnon Story

I'll close by telling you an "Amnon Story" that occurred in my ministry many years ago. I was concerned about a young man (we'll call him Tom) in our youth group who was running around with the wrong crowd. Tom was a good guy, raised in a good family; but an intense desire to be accepted and considered cool by a certain group of friends was slowly changing him.

Early one morning I got a frantic phone call from Tom's mother asking me to come quickly to their home. Police had arrived at 6 a.m. and taken Tom into custody. The night before Tom was out with four of these friends just "cruising around." One of them got the idea to rob a convenience store out in an isolated area.

Tom knew this was wrong and found himself in a tight spot. He told his friends he wanted to go home, and when they couldn't talk him out of his decision, they reluctantly took him home to the tune of, "Chicken. You can't be a real man like us, can you?" Tom went to bed, relieved that he had found a way out of this trouble.

Only he hadn't.

The friends broke into the convenience store shortly after midnight and stole several items. As the friends were leaving the scene of the robbery, one of them noticed that in his haste to get out of the car, Tom had left his coat. To get Tom back for his "cowardice," they tossed his coat into the store. What they didn't know was that Tom's mother had written his name inside the coat, so it didn't take long for the police to track him down.

Tom eventually was sent to a juvenile detention center for his punishment. The other four boys (like Amnon) were never arrested or punished because there was no direct evidence linking them to the crime. So, Tom was serving time for a crime he didn't commit while his "friends" who committed the crime were free.

Tom had done nothing wrong or had he? The reality is he had made the same wrong choice Amnon made – he had chosen the wrong kind of friends!

Go back for a moment and look at Amnon's tombstone: "Amnon had a friend. He was a very shrewd man."

Amnon had a great family. He had a great father, a man after God's own heart. He had a great future ahead of him. But he also had the wrong kind of friend, and that made all the difference in the world!

I Have Learned That...

Let this Bible story sink deep into your soul. Who are your friends? What are they teaching you? Are they an asset or a liability? Are they influencing you for good or bad? Will they help you get to heaven?

All of these questions are important, for I have learned that friends can make you or break you!

Talking Back

1. How would you define a true friend?

2. Read Proverbs 27:17. What does this verse mean?

3. What was Amnon's mistake? What irritates you about Jonadab?

4. Discuss the various ways your friends can be your greatest asset or your greatest liability.

5. How do you choose your friends? What do you look for and what do you avoid?

Exercising Your Faith

1. Write a letter of appreciation, thanksgiving or encouragement to your best friends. It will bless you and them!

2. Reach out to someone who looks like he needs a friend. You might really make an incredible difference in that person's life.

Life Can Be Tough, But God Will Help Us Overcome

Have you ever had a bad day? We all have them at one time or another. Consider the bad day this construction worker experienced. He had to file a detailed report on an accident form for his insurance company and this is what he wrote:

> When I got to the building, I found that the hurricane had knocked off some bricks around the top. So I rigged up a beam with a pulley at the top of the building and hoisted up a couple barrels full of bricks. When I had fixed the damaged area, there were a lot of bricks left over. Then I went to the bottom and began releasing the line. Unfortunately, the barrel of bricks was much heavier than I was – and before I knew what was happening, the barrel started coming down, jerking me up.
>
> I decided to hang on since I was too far off the ground by then to jump, and halfway up I met the barrel of bricks coming down fast. I received a hard blow on my shoulder. I then continued to the top, banging my head against the beam and getting my fingers pinched and jammed in the pulley. When the barrel hit the ground hard, it burst its bottom, allowing the bricks to spill out.

I now was heavier than the barrel. So I started down again at high speed. Halfway down I met the barrel coming up fast and received severe injuries to my shins. When I hit the ground, I landed on the pile of spilled bricks, getting several painful cuts and deep bruises. At this point I must have lost my presence of mind, because I let go of my grip on the line. The barrel came down fast – giving me another hard blow on my head and putting me in the hospital. I respectfully request sick leave.

Now that's what I call a bad day!

At times in your life, you will find yourself having a bad day – or even a bad week, month or year! Life can be tough, no doubt about it, but neither should there be any doubt that God will help us overcome tough times!

Tough Problems

The first few verses of 1 Peter address people dealing with tough problems:

In this [salvation] you greatly rejoice, though now for a little while you may have to suffer grief in all kinds of trials. These have come so that your faith – of greater worth than gold, which perishes even though refined by fire – may be proved genuine and may result in praise, glory, and honor when Jesus Christ is revealed. Though you have not seen him, you love him; and even though you do not see him now, you believe in him and are filled with an inexpressible and glorious joy, for you are receiving the goal of your faith, the salvation of your souls (1 Peter 1:6-9).

Those trials are problems or adversity. Whether you face family problems, friend problems, money problems, relationship problems, school problems, or work problems, Peter reminds us of some important principles for overcoming problems.

■ *The problem is only "for a little while."* When you are going through a crisis, it sometimes seems as though time stands still and there is no way out. But Peter reminds us our problems are only temporary; they are not going to last forever.

Richard Carlson wrote a book that topped the best-seller's list for months titled: *Don't Sweat the Small Stuff ... and It's All Small Stuff.* When we look at our problems, they don't seem small; they seem huge. When we look at our problems, they don't seem temporary; they seem permanent. But that's only because our perspective is distorted. If you change your perspective, you might just solve your problem.

I read an article about two young men who had totally different perspectives on being jilted by their girlfriends. One jumped off a bridge, leaving behind a note that read, "I'm jumping off this bridge because the only girl I ever loved is mad at me and broke up with me, and I think this is the only way out." The other young man, when his girlfriend jilted him, wrote of his heartache in a country song. The tune became a hit and netted him thousands of dollars in royalties and a new career! When your romance fails and your heart is broken, don't jump off a bridge – write a song and get rich!

Seriously, proper perspective will help you realize that your problems are temporary.

■ *You can rejoice even in the midst of the problem.* "In this you greatly rejoice, though now for a little while you may have had to suffer grief in all kinds of trials" (1 Peter 1:6). There are still blessings to count and reasons to rejoice even while we are facing problems. In fact, Peter listed some of them in verses 3-5. We have:

- Great mercy;
- New birth;
- Living hope;
- An inheritance that can never perish, spoil or fade;
- Shielded by God's power.

Whenever you are facing problems, instead of allowing them to overwhelm you, why not try overcoming them by rejoicing? Get out a pen and paper and write down all your reasons to rejoice, and you'll probably begin to send your problem to the recycle bin!

■ *The problem can help you grow stronger in Christ.* In 1 Peter 1:7, Peter said our problems can strengthen our faith and prove it to be genuine. You cannot have spiritual growth without problems. I wish that pleasure caused growth, but it seldom does. Athletes who do weight training have a slogan: "No pain – no gain." That's not just a nice slogan, it's a biblical truth! No one likes to struggle with problems, but with the attitude of faith, you can look upon them as opportunities to grow.

I once read about a little boy who was playing outside and found a cocoon attached to a leaf that had fallen to the ground. He took the cocoon to his room and watched as a butterfly began its struggle to emerge from it. It was a long, hard struggle and it seemed to the boy that the insect was stuck and making almost no progress. Finally, he decided to help the butterfly out of its difficulty.

He took a pair of scissors and snipped off a portion of the cocoon's restrictive covering to make the opening larger. The butterfly crawled out, but with its weakened wings that's all it ever did – crawl. What the boy didn't understand was that the butterfly's struggle to get through the tiny opening was necessary in order to force colorful, life-giving fluids into its wings so that it would be strong enough to fly. Without the struggle, the wings never developed.

In a similar sense, without the struggle of problems, our spiritual wings never grow properly. Struggle provides us the resistance necessary to develop faith and test the genuineness of our walk with Christ.

Tough Thorns

In 2 Corinthians 12, Paul discusses what he called, "a thorn in my flesh" (v. 7). What is truly amazing is that he described his thorn as a gift from God:

> To keep me from becoming conceited because of these surpassingly great revelations, there was given me a thorn in my flesh, a messenger of Satan, to torment me. Three times, I pleaded with the Lord to take it away from me. But he said to me, "My grace is sufficient for you, for my power is made perfect in weakness." Therefore, I will boast all the more gladly about my weaknesses, so that Christ's power may rest on me. That is why, for Christ's sake, I delight in weaknesses, in insults, in hardships, in persecutions, in difficulties. For when I am weak, then I am strong (2 Corinthians 12:7-10).

We all will have thorns in our lives – physical (which apparently was Paul's), emotional and spiritual thorns. They are constantly there jabbing at our lives, pricking and poking us, keeping us scratched and scarred with discomfort. It might be some physical characteristic that we don't like about ourselves. It might be a disease. It might be a handicap or limitation. Or it might be a person or group of people. It might be self-inflicted or thrust upon us, or some combination of both.

The question is not, "Will we have thorns?" We will. The question is, "Will we find God's power and grace to deal with our thorns?" Perhaps understanding why we have thorns will help us deal with them appropriately. There are three primary reasons Christians have thorns.

■ *We are human and live in a fallen world.* Since Adam and Eve sinned in the Garden of Eden, the world has been increasingly full of sin, and we live in the fallout. A drunk driver hits another car causing death or injury. A father abuses his daughter, who suffers because of his sinful choice. A teenager is promiscuous, and it leads to an illegitimate birth or a sexually transmitted disease. These sinful choices and actions may cause innocent people to suffer.

We must remember that if God eliminated our freewill choice, He would be eliminating our choice to love and know Him, which is our very reason for being. It would also eliminate our choice to love and care for others.

■ *We have thorns as a result of our own bad choices.* Because of the choices a person makes, a smoker risks cancer, an alcoholic risks liver disease, a sexually promiscuous person risks sexual diseases such as herpes or AIDs. An angry God does not cause those thorns – the risks are related to the choices.

■ *Thorns can be a tool God uses to make us spiritually strong.* This, of course, is what Paul said about his thorn in the flesh. Sometimes thorns are not a punishment but a training ground. Parents sometimes allow their children to go through some hurt to build their character. If children never experienced any adversity, they would grow up to be maladjusted and insecure people. God, our heavenly parent, allows us to have some thorns to help us grow spiritually. The Hebrew writer put it this way:

> Our fathers disciplined us for a little while as they thought best; but God disciplines us for our good, that we may share in his holiness. No discipline seems pleasant at the time, but painful. Later on, however, it produces a harvest of righteousness and peace for those who have been trained by it (Hebrews 12:10-11).

Paul prayed fervently three times for God to remove his thorn. But there are times when God answers our prayer for thorn removal with, "No, it will ultimately be better for you if you keep your thorn. My grace is sufficient for you. Although you may not see it or understand it now, your thorn is good for you and is making you stronger. No pain, no gain."

I read about an airplane pilot who announced over the intercom: "We have lost one of our four engines. But don't worry; we'll be able to make it to our destination with three engines, and perhaps you'll be re-assured to know there are four preachers on board to pray."

One passenger leaned over to the stewardess and said, "I'd rather have four engines and three preachers, wouldn't you?"

Most of the time we'd rather rely on our power and not have to pray or rely on God. But thorns force us to rely on God, and pray and trust that His grace will be sufficient and His power will be made perfect in our weakness.

A Tough Adversary

Frankly, a major reason we have tough times is the evil work of Satan, whose mission is clearly defined in the Bible.

> The thief comes only to steal and kill and destroy (John 10:10).

> Your enemy the devil prowls around like a roaring lion look-ing for someone to devour (1 Peter 5:8).

The good news is Jesus has overcome our adversary, Satan, and He will help us overcome him, too. Jesus said, "In this world you will have trouble. But take heart! I have overcome the world" (John 16:33).

I once heard a dynamic parable of the judgment that perfectly illus-trates how Christ has overcome the world:

At the end of time, all the people who had ever lived were brought before the throne of God to be judged. Most of them were mumbling and grumbling, prepared to make complaints before God.

One group was made up of Jews who had suffered great persecution throughout history, particularly in the Holocaust. Some had died in gas chambers or concentration camps. They cried out, "Who is God, that He should be our judge? How could God judge us? What could He know of our suffering?"

The next group were slaves who had suffered all kinds of human indignities. They shouted, "Who is God, that He should be our judge? What does He know of mistreatment?"

Then there were poor folks – workers who had never been able to make ends meet. There were homeless people who had no place to lay their heads. There were sick and diseased people, and sufferers of all kind, each voicing their complaint against God.

"How could God judge us?" they said over and over again. How fortunate God is to live in heaven where there are no tears, no worries, no fears, no diseases, no sufferings, no deaths. So they appointed a commission to draw up the case against God. Their conclusion was, before God could judge them, He must walk a mile in their shoes and endure what they had endured. So they sentenced God to live on earth as a man, to submit to the painful, tough life of mankind. They shouted out:

> Let Him be born a Jew!
> Let Him be born poor!
> Let Him be rejected by His own people!
> Let Him have no home of His own to lay His head!
> Give Him hard work to do!
> Let Him be betrayed by His friends!
> Let Him be the victim of racial profiling, be arrested, falsely charged, and convicted by a cowardly judge!
> Let Him be abandoned by His friends!
> Let Him be tortured!
> Let Him be lonely!
> Let Him die at the hands of His enemies!

As each group announced its sentence to God, cheers of approval went up from the crowd. Then suddenly, there was quiet. Not a word or a sound. No one moved. For everyone suddenly realized God has already served that exact sentence through His Son, Jesus Christ!

We have a Savior who speaks to us not from an easy chair but from a cross! At that old rugged cross He won the battle over Satan and sin and He shares that victory with us:

> For everyone born of God overcomes the world. This is the victory that has overcome the world, even our faith. Who is it that overcomes the world? Only he who believes that Jesus is the Son of God (1 John 5:4-5).

I Have Learned That...

So, yes, our tough adversary, Satan, will place tough problems and tough thorns in our pathway, but I have learned through the Bible and through life experiences that although life can be tough, God will help us overcome!

Talking Back

1. Read 1 Peter 1:6-9. What can we find to rejoice about even in the midst of tough problems?

2. Discuss the slogan, "No pain – no gain." What does that mean to you?

3. Do you have a thorn in the flesh? How do you deal with it?

4. How can problems or thorns actually make you stronger spiritually?

5. How is Jesus our example in overcoming our problems and thorns?

Exercising Your Faith

1. Make two lists:

   a. My problem or thorn is ...

   b. The way God can help me with my problem or thorn is ...

   Keep the lists near you and concentrate on God's help rather than the problem.

2. Follow the example of Jesus. Get your mind off your own problems or thorns by going and helping someone else, preferably someone less fortunate than yourself.

"A Cheerful Heart Is Like Good Medicine, But a Crushed Spirit Dries Up the Bones"

I attended David Lipscomb High School and University where daily chapel services are required. I estimate that I attended approximately 1,000 chapel services and I remember only four of them. Three of them are irrelevant for my purposes in this chapter, but the other is one of my motivations behind this life lesson.

The football coach and senior Bible teacher at Lipscomb High School was a firm disciplinarian and a master motivator. He was known for giving serious, challenging chapel talks. But one day he got up and told a joke. Then another joke, followed by a very funny story. This went on for 20 minutes, one funny joke and story after another. No scriptures, no outline, no moral lesson – just 20 minutes of hilarious jokes and stories.

Abruptly he sat down. About a minute passed and no one said a word – no song, no announcements, no closing prayer, just awkward silence. Then, the coach went back to the podium and said something like this: "This has been a heavy week here at school. I know there have been a lot of problems and troubled hearts. So I thought it would be helpful if we just laughed today. And by the way, I think that's what God would have us do, because Proverbs 17:22 says, "A cheerful heart is good medicine, but a crushed spirit dries up the bones."

And with that we were dismissed. I was one of the ones with a troubled heart that day, and I can tell you I don't think I've ever had a speech or sermon minister to me like that day. What's more, I don't think I'd ever heard that verse before that day, but it has blessed my heart hundreds of times since that one. An important real life lesson I've learned is that a "cheerful heart is good medicine, but a crushed spirit dries up the bones."

Have you ever been sick with the flu and felt miserable until the doctor prescribed an antibiotic, and shortly after taking it you began to feel much better? The Bible teaches that a cheerful heart is God's medicine to heal our spiritual and emotional sicknesses! There is divine healing power in laughter, joy and a cheerful spirit.

According to a legend told by ancient Greeks, the gods on Mount Olympus held a council to decide where they could hide the secret to happiness so that when it was found, the people would appreciate it more. "Let us hide it on the highest mountain. It will never be found there," one god replied. "Let us bury it deep into the earth," another suggested. Still others suggested that the secret to happiness be buried in the depths of the deepest ocean.

Finally, one of the gods came up with a solution: "Let us hide the secret to happiness in the last place that anyone would ever look, a place they will come to when all other possibilities are exhausted. We will hide the secret to happiness deep within the people themselves."

For centuries, people have searched for the secret of happiness, but most never realize that it lies deep within each of us, for as God's Word says, "A cheerful heart is good medicine, but a crushed spirit dries up the bones."

Other scriptures teach the same truth:

A happy heart makes the face cheerful, but heartache crushes the spirit (Proverbs 15:13).

All the days of the oppressed are wretched, but the cheerful heart has a continual feast (Proverbs 15:15).

A cheerful look brings joy to the heart, and good news gives health to the bones (Proverbs 15:30).

A man's spirit sustains him in sickness, but a crushed spirit who can bear? (Proverbs 18:14).

It is a documented scientific fact that people who laugh a lot, on the average, live longer than those who don't. When you enjoy a good hearty laugh, muscles in the abdomen, chest and shoulders contract while heart rate and blood pressure increase, the same as in exercise. When you stop laughing, heartbeat and blood pressure dip below normal which is a sign of reduced stress. So, literally, "He who laughs, lasts."

The Power of a Cheerful Heart

Let me give you a couple of well-known examples – one a movie, the other a book. *Patch Adams* was a 1999 movie about the true story of a compassionate but outrageous doctor who risks his career by defying the medical profession with his firm belief that laughter is contagious and has healing powers. Dr. Patch Adams, an Arlington, Va., physician who charges no money (his income is based on donations and fees from radio/television), carries no malpractice insurance, and uses laughter and friendship as his chief healing devices. The real Dr. Adams has been quoted as saying, "The best therapy is being happy. All the other things doctors can do are at best aids. Health is typically defined as the absence of disease. To me, health is a happy, vibrant, exuberant life every single day of your life. Anything less is a certain amount of disease."

Adams has helped heal a great many sick people with his philosophy. Why should we be surprised? God's Word says, "A cheerful heart is good medicine, but a crushed spirit dries up the bones."

In 1964, Norman Cousins was the powerful and influential editor of *The Saturday Evening Post*. Diagnosed with the crippling and incurable degenerative disease of *ankylosing spondylitis*, Cousins decided he was going to take control of his own treatment. He shunned ordinary treatment and opted instead for big doses of laughter. He checked himself out of a dreary hospital and into a hotel room where he could watch comedy movies and TV shows around the clock.

Cousins discovered that laughter gave him some relief from the pain that kept him in agony and unable to sleep. Away from the hospital, his condition kept improving. Tests were run "before laughter" and "after laughter," and they always showed a marked improvement following his laughter sessions. Cousins was convinced that laughter literally releases a healing potion into our bodies and that it was the primary reason for his recovery. His best-selling book, *Anatomy of an Illness*, is an inspiring account of his discovery.

Cousins helped millions of suffering people find some relief from their pain with his book. Why should we be surprised? God's Word says, "A cheerful heart is good medicine, but a crushed spirit dries up the bones."

I'm not suggesting that you disregard all medical advice and attempt to laugh yourself out of every illness. Nor do I recommend you throw away the Tylenol in the medicine cabinet. But I do want you to recognize the power of a cheerful heart.

It bothers me that the Christian life is so often presented as a drab, somber march. We sometimes act like the gospel, the "good news," is bad news by our somber spirits!

Christians should certainly take life seriously, but I don't believe for one minute God wants us to be somber – to have a gloomy, dismal attitude. To the contrary, he wants us to have a cheerful heart.

I was watching the game show *Family Feud* on television one day, and the question came up, "What is the most boring place to be?" I feared what was coming and, sure enough, the number one answer was church. It ought not be that way! Christians are to spread the good news with good cheer that is the result of a cheerful heart!

It's okay to laugh. It's okay to enjoy our faith. In fact, laughter, humor and joy are gifts from God endorsed by the Scriptures.

The Benefits of a Cheerful Heart

How does a cheerful heart help us?

■ *A cheerful heart helps our outlook on life.* Wherever Jesus looked, He saw God at work. The flowers in a field reminded Him that God loves and cares for us (Matthew 6:28-30). The birds in the air reminded Him that God feeds us (v. 26). Jesus understood that one of the secrets of a cheerful heart is to see God everywhere one looks, which teaches an important principle: Your up-look will determine your outlook.

I heard about a man and his wife on a long trip pulling into a full-service gas station. After the station attendant had washed the car's windshield, the man in the car shouted to the attendant, "It's still dirty. Wash it again." So the attendant washed it a second time. After a few minutes, the man in the car angrily said, "It's still dirty. Don't you know how to wash a windshield?" Just then the man's wife reached over, removed her husband's glasses, and cleaned them with a tissue. She then placed them back on her husband and – the windshield was clean!

What do you see when you look out of your windshield on the world? Do you start the morning with a cheerful heart that is like good medicine or with a crushed spirit that dries up the bones? When your outlook is one of fear and unhappiness, that's what you will experience. But when your outlook begins with a cheerful heart and a determination to look up to the Lord for His blessings, your faith will grow and your joy will multiply!

■ *A cheerful heart helps us not to judge others so quickly.* A story is told in *Reader's Digest* about a lady who was shopping in a mall. She decided to take a break, so she bought a newspaper and a candy bar and sat down on a bench to relax and enjoy her paper and candy. She started looking through the newspaper, and then she broke off a corner of the candy bar and popped it into her mouth. A nicely dressed man was sitting next to her, and much to her surprise he suddenly reached down, took a piece of the candy bar, and popped it into his mouth!

The woman was stunned, but she figured, "I'll ignore it this once." So she took another piece of the candy bar – and he took another piece. Then he beat her to the punch and took another piece before she could grab one. By this time she was enraged. She grabbed the candy bar, flashed the man a hostile look, and threw it in the garbage can, storming off through the mall.

A little later in the day, she saw the same man standing in front of the mall bakery with a donut in his hand. Later she said, "I don't know what possessed me. I'm not this kind of person usually, but I couldn't resist the temptation. I grabbed his wrist, took a big bite out of the donut, and walked away." Then she confessed, "When I got home, I put my things down, opened my purse – and there was my unwrapped candy bar!"

She had been eating his candy bar all along!

We are quick to judge and so prone to misunderstand each other. We get terribly mixed up, and we make relationships tense and complex. If only we would think and act with a cheerful heart, we would not be so quick to judge others!

■ *A cheerful heart will help us learn to laugh at ourselves.* A secret to a cheerful heart is to accept who you are, made in God's image, and not take yourself so seriously that you cannot laugh at yourself.

Clark Kent Ervin was a bright young African-American lawyer who graduated from Harvard Law School and practiced law with one of the nation's finest law firms. When he was in his late 20s, President George Bush asked him to come to Washington and work in a new program as part of the White House staff.

As Ervin was packing up his old office, his secretary buzzed him and told him *Time* magazine was on the line. Ervin said, "I wasn't surprised – after all, I was going to Washington, and evidently *Time* had heard about me and wanted to interview me." He told his secretary to tell them he was not available at the moment, but to please call back in 5 minutes. He wanted some time to think of some quotable quotes and impressive statements that would make him look good in the interview. Exactly 5 minutes later, *Time* called back, and Ervin was ready with his brilliant statements. This conversation took place:

"Is this Clark Ervin?"

"Yes."

"Is this Clark Kent Ervin?"

"Yes."

"Well, this is *Time* magazine calling, and we just wanted to know if you wanted to renew your subscription!"

What makes that funny story even more enjoyable is that Clark Kent Ervin tells it on himself. He is able to laugh at himself, and that is a characteristic of a cheerful heart.

■ *A cheerful heart comes from serving others and sharing with others.* You don't get a cheerful heart by going out and looking for it – a cheerful heart naturally comes as a result of service to others.

The most miserable people I know are selfish people, people who think mostly or only of themselves. On the other hand, the happiest people I know are those who think of others and serve others. Selfishness always smothers happiness, but service fills us with joy and good cheer.

The best example I know of this principle occurs every year on Dec. 25 and the days leading up to Christmas. For several days people scurry around looking for gifts for others, thinking of others, singing songs of joy and faith, volunteering in service projects, and sharing good cheer.

And, as a result, they are happier and more fulfilled.

Then, suddenly, on Dec. 26 all that serving, sacrifice and gift-seeking stops. We stop thinking about others and doing things for others, and we return to thinking about ourselves and our perceived needs. And the result is predictable – we are not as happy and cheerful. That shouldn't surprise us, for Jesus plainly said, "It is more blessed to give than to receive" (Acts 20:35). The more we give to others and serve others, the more cheerful we will be!

Like any medicine, the medicine of a cheerful heart must be applied. Our world is full of so much pain, trouble and sorrow. We need God's medicine of a cheerful heart to help us make it through; and we need the medicine of a cheerful heart to help others make it through.

I Have Learned That...

I challenge you to try God's spiritual medicine, a cheerful heart, for I have learned that a "cheerful heart is good medicine, but a crushed spirit dries up the bones."

Talking Back

1. Read Proverbs 17:22. Discuss what that verse means. Can you remember times when it has been true in your life?

2. Look up the definitions of sober and somber. What is the difference between Christians being sober and being somber?

3. Have you ever seen anything really funny happen in church? If so, describe it.

4. Contrast a "cheerful heart" with a "crushed spirit." What are the defining characteristics of each?

5. Why are selfish people the most miserable people? How does a cheerful heart come from serving others and sharing with others?

Exercising Your Faith

1. Have a "Cheerful Heart Day." Spend a whole day watching funny movies, reading funny books, or telling good (clean) jokes. You are guaranteed to find yourself more joyful at the end of the day.

2. Memorize Proverbs 17:22. Repeat it several times a day or pray it to remind you of its truth.

It Is Foolish To Major in Minors And Minor In Majors

An expert on time management drove home a point on setting priorities with this illustration. He lifted a one-gallon, wide-mouthed Mason jar and set it on a table in front of him. He then placed, one at a time, 12 fist-sized rocks into the jar. When no more rocks would fit, he asked the audience if they believed the jar to be full. They said they did.

He then reached under the table and produced a bucket of gravel. He scooped it into the jar and then shook it, thus causing the gravel to fill the spots between the rocks. He asked the same question again, and this time there were mixed replies.

He took another box from under the table that was filled with sand. Dumping it in, it filled the gaps between the gravel and rocks. He asked the same question for a third time and no one said anything.

He then pulled out a pitcher of water and began pouring it in until the jar was filled to the brim. He then said that the point of the illustration is simple: "If you don't put the big rocks in first, you will never get them in at all. Do you know what the big rocks are in your life?"

That's a good question. Do you know what the big rocks, the most important priorities, in your life are? And are you putting them first in your life? Ask yourself these questions:

- What is really important to me?
- What do I spend most of my free time doing?

- What do I think about most often?
- What do I spend my extra money on?
- What do I treasure?
- What's in the top few spots on my priority list?

People often major in minors (things that ultimately aren't very important) and minor in majors (things that ultimately are very important).

A few years ago there was a very funny movie titled *City Slickers*. The plot of the film revolves around three New York City men who decide to spend a vacation together finding themselves on a cattle drive out West. A tough old cowboy named Curly leads the cattle drive. One day Curly has a conversation with Mitch: "You city folk – you worry a lot. You spend 50 weeks getting knots in your rope and you think two weeks out here will untie them for you. None of you get it." Curly paused a moment and asked, "You know what the secret to life is?"

"No. What?" says Mitch.

"One thing. Just one thing. You stick to that, and everything else don't mean nothing."

As Curly rides off on his horse, Mitch yells, "That's great, but what's the one thing?"

Curly turns and says, "That's what you've got to figure out."

Curly was right. That's exactly what Jesus tells us. Only one thing in life really matters ultimately. If you can find that one thing and focus on it, everything else falls into place. According to Jesus, the one thing is to "seek first his kingdom and his righteousness, and all these things will be given to you as well" (Matthew 6:33).

The Minors That We Major In

What are some of the minors that we treat as if they were majors?

■ *Riches.* I read about a young man who said that when he was in college he asked some of his fellow students if they had a major.

They said, "Accounting."

He asked, "So you like figures and numbers?"

Several of them replied, "No, not particularly."

"Well, why are you majoring in accounting?"

They replied, "That is where the jobs are. That's where you can really make some money."

The young man thought that it was odd for people to spend most of their waking hours for 30 to 40 years working on a job they dislike just to make a little more money. They would spend much of their lives being miserable to make themselves a little more money. It seems foolish, but people do it.

As we discussed in chapter 6, there is nothing wrong with riches. In fact, God may bless you with wealth. But there *is* something wrong with seeking wealth first, or even second or third! "For the love of money is a root of all kinds of evil. Some people, eager for money, have wandered from the faith and pierced themselves with many griefs" (1 Timothy 6:10).

If you believe that riches are the ticket to happiness and fulfillment, you are in for a big fall. Wealth is a minor, not a major!

■ *Beauty.* Beauty is so fleeting. A Miss America from the 1960s may not be considered beautiful today.

We buy designer clothes and brand-name cosmetics. We get face lifts and tummy tucks. We buy into Satan's lie that external beauty will make us happy and successful. But the truth is, beauty can do no more than complement what's inside the container. Proverbs 31:30 is right: "Charm is deceptive, and beauty is fleeting; but a woman who fears the Lord is to be praised."

■ *Fame.* History proves over and over again that fame is very fickle. Those who cheer one day may boo the next. Those who were saying "Hallelujah!" to Jesus as He entered Jerusalem one week were shouting, "Crucify Him!" the next week. You had better live for something more meaningful than temporary popularity.

■ *Selfish desires.* We live in a me-first culture. We are often conditioned to be self-centered and look out for No. 1 by TV programs, movies, magazines and advertising.

Even the disciples of Jesus were tempted with this me-first, selfish attitude:

> An argument started among the disciples as to which of them would be the greatest. Jesus, knowing their thoughts, took a little child and had him stand beside them. Then he said to them, "Whoever welcomes this little child in my name welcomes me; and whoever welcomes me welcomes the one who

sent me. For he who is least among you all – he is the greatest" (Luke 9:46-48).

On another occasion, Jesus said, "The greatest among you will be your servant. For whoever exalts himself will be humbled, and whoever humbles himself will be exalted" (Matthew 23:11-12).

Seeking our own pleasure is the road to loneliness, not happiness. Instead, we should, "Do nothing out of selfish ambition or vain conceit, but in humility consider others better than yourselves. Each of you should look not only to your own interests, but also to the interests of others" (Philippians 2:3-4).

The Majors That We Minor In

Let's do this top-10 style, with number one always being the same, and the other "majors" moving around from time to time in terms of priority, depending upon circumstances.

■ *No. 10: Love.* Loving God and loving others are the two greatest commands, according to Jesus (Matthew 22:34-40). In fact, love is the identifying badge of a Christian:

> A new command I give you: Love one another. As I have loved you, so you must love one another. All men will know that you are my disciples if you love one another (John 13:34-35).

And, of course, in the great love chapter, 1 Corinthians 13, love was identified as priority number one:

> And now these three remain: faith, hope, and love. But the greatest of these is love (v. 13).

■ *No. 9: School or work.* School is a priority during your teen years because it provides you with the education and the discipline to succeed later in life. If you doubt the value of education consider this – the latest statistics show that college graduates make, on the average, $13,000 a year more than those without a college degree. Over the course of a career that amounts to more than a half-million dollars! Should you perhaps re-think school as one of your priorities? At school or at work, remember the words of Colossians 3:23: "Whatever you do, work at it with all your heart, as working for the Lord, not for men, since you know that you will receive an inheritance from the Lord as a reward. It is the Lord Christ you are serving."

■ *No. 8: Health.* Your body is the dwelling place of God.

> Do you not know that your body is a temple of the Holy Spirit, who is in you, whom you have received from God? You are not your own; you were bought at a price. Therefore honor God with your body (1 Corinthians 6:19-20).

One reason we should not abuse our bodies with drugs, alcohol, tobacco and sexual immorality is because we are defiling the temple of the Holy Spirit! Another more practical reason is not to destroy our health – after all, this is the only body we will ever have! Take care of your body and your health while you are young and while you can – you won't regret it.

■ *No. 7: Friends.* People are a priority! Especially people who love us and are close to us, our friends.

> A friend loves at all times, and a brother is born for adversity (Proverbs 17:17).

> Perfume and incense bring joy to the heart, and the pleasantness of one's friend springs from his earnest counsel. Do not forsake your friend (Proverbs 27:9-10).

Don't take friendship lightly! Faithful friends deserve to be a major in our lives, not a minor.

■ *No. 6: Service.* Someone once said, "Service is the rent you pay for the space you occupy on earth." The Bible teaches that service should be a priority for a Christian.

> [W]hoever wants to become great among you must be your servant, and whoever wants to be first must be your slave – just as the Son of Man did not come to be served, but to serve, and to give his life as a ransom for many (Matthew 20:26-28).

> Therefore, I urge you, brothers, in view of God's mercy, to offer your bodies as living sacrifices, holy and pleasing to God – this is your spiritual act of worship (Romans 12:1).

Each one should use whatever gift he has received to serve others, faithfully administering God's grace in its various forms (1 Peter 4:10).

If serving others wasn't too good for Jesus, it certainly shouldn't be for us! When people ask WWJD (What Would Jesus Do?), we know the answer – He would serve! And so should we make service a priority!

■ *No. 5: Prayer.* Spending time alone with God in prayer must be a major priority in our lives. Talk to God about your concerns and problems. Seek His guidance for important decisions you're making. Express your gratitude for all the good things in your life:

Do not be anxious about anything, but in everything, by prayer and petition, with thanksgiving, present your requests to God (Philippians 4:6).

Is any one of you in trouble? He should pray … .Therefore confess your sins to each other and pray for each other so that you may be healed. The prayer of a righteous man is powerful and effective (James 5:13, 16).

■ *No. 4: Bible study.* If you want to grow spiritually, you will need to devote yourself to learning and applying the teachings of God's Word.

How can a young man keep his way pure? By living according to your word (Psalm 119:9).

Your word is a lamp to my feet and a light for my path (Psalm 119:105).

Like newborn babies, crave pure spiritual milk, so that by it you may grow up in your salvation (1 Peter 2:2).

Living in a materialistic society as we do, we are constantly bombarded with non-Christian influences from television, movies, music and magazines. To counter the influences of these messages, we simply must make time for reading and studying God's Word.

■ *No. 3: Church.* The church is the body of Christ (of which He is the head) and the family of God. Hebrews 10:24-25 explains what we are to do in the church and why we are to do it:

> And let us consider how we may spur one another on toward love and good deeds. Let us not give up meeting together, as some are in the habit of doing, but let us encourage one another – and all the more as you see the Day approaching.

What we are to do is simple: Go to church regularly to worship God, fellowship with other Christians and grow in faith. The church helps us accomplish these goals because it provides the place where we encourage one another and spur one another on toward love and good deeds.

If you think about it, the church is the only institution dealing with all of the ultimate issues of life: death, eternity, marriage, parenting, purpose and meaning, relationships, identity, proper self-image, forgiveness, grace, heaven, hell. Only the church deals with all these big rocks – and when people need help in these all-important areas, where do they usually go? To the church, as they can and should! Make the church a priority in your life.

■ *No. 2: Family.* Your family should always be a major priority. The Bible says,

> Children, obey your parents in the Lord, for this is right. "Honor your father and mother" – which is the first commandment with a promise – "that it may go well with you and that you may enjoy long life on the earth" (Ephesians 6:1-2).

Throughout life, you may have lots of friends, better health, more money, and other jobs, but you have only one family. Once it is gone, that's it. You have only one set of parents and grandparents, and one group of siblings. Don't neglect them now and regret it later.

■ *No. 1: God.* No discussion about the first priority is needed. Jesus made clear the Lord is priority No. 1:

> Hearing that Jesus had silenced the Sadducees, the Pharisees got together. One of them, an expert in the law, tested him with this question: "Teacher, which is the greatest commandment in the Law?" Jesus replied, "'Love the Lord your God with all your heart and with all your soul and with all your mind.' This is the first and greatest commandment" (Matthew 22:36-38).

And, of course, the first of the Ten Commandments was: "You shall have no other gods before me" (Exodus 20:3).

There you have it – a top 10 list of priorities, big rocks, for any follower of Jesus. Are you majoring in the minors or minoring in the majors? If so, begin now to set your priorities straight.

One of my favorite movies is *Field of Dreams*, a touching parable about fathers and sons, reconciliation and forgiveness, and having proper priorities. The main character is driven to find an old doctor. The doctor, as a young man, had been a professional baseball player. He had made it to the major leagues but had only played in the game for one inning before his career ended. He didn't even get a chance to bat. The rest of his life was spent as a small-town doctor whose love for his patients was legendary.

In the movie, the old doctor is offered a chance to return, magically, to his youth and to re-enter the major leagues – but if he goes back, he cannot return to his life as a doctor. It was his chance at fame and to prove himself as good enough for the big leagues. But the old doctor declined. The main character says, "But you only got to play 5 minutes in the big leagues. That's a tragedy!" To which the old doctor replies, "No, if I had only gotten to be a doctor for 5 minutes, that would have been a tragedy!"

I Have Learned That...

The doctor had his priorities straight. Do you? I hope so because I have learned that it is foolish to major in minors and minor in majors.

Talking Back

1. What are the most important priorities in your life right now? Why are they your priorities?

2. Which of the minors mentioned in this chapter are you tempted to major in?

3. Which of the majors mentioned in this chapter are you tempted to minor in?

4. Why is the church a big rock, a major priority, or why should it be?

5. What practical things can you do to make sure you are majoring in the majors, not the minors?

Exercising Your Faith

1. Make a list of the top 10 priorities in your life right now – be honest. Then make a separate list rating the Top 10 priorities mentioned in the chapter – how you would honestly rank them right now in our life.

2. Ask someone – a family member, a Christian friend, a youth minister, etc. – to hold you accountable to living up to the major priorities of life. Give them permission to ask you tough questions about your priorities.

Winners Don't Quit and Quitters Don't Win

During the days of the California gold rush, two brothers from Kansas sold everything they had and moved west to prospect for gold. As luck would have it, inside a small fault in the ground, they discovered a vein of the shiny, valuable ore. So they staked a claim and proceeded to get the gold ore out of the mine.

Things were going fine at first, but suddenly the vein that had been producing gold ore for them ended. They gave up in disgust and decided that their pot of gold was no longer there. The brothers sold their equipment and claim rights for a few hundred dollars and went home to Kansas.

The man who bought the claim hired an engineer to examine the area near where the brothers had been mining. The engineer advised him to continue digging in the same spot where the brothers had stopped. And there, just 3 feet deeper, the new owner hit one of the largest gold finds of the entire gold rush! Just a little more persistence and the two brothers would have been multi-millionaires themselves.

Most people give up too easily and too quickly. They will try something for a while and when it appears that the payoff is taking too long, they will quit and go look for something they think will be easier. But often, the difference between success and failure is taking that one extra step – digging 3 feet deeper!

Paul wrote, "Let us not become weary in doing good, for at the proper time we will reap a harvest if we do not give up" (Galatians 6:9). Those two brothers from Kansas should have listened to this biblical advice.

In practical terms, Paul is saying, "Hang in there." "Finish the Christian race." "Don't give up; don't quit." "Persevere and you will be rewarded."

This biblical counsel is so important for the times in which we live because quitting is so commonplac. The "I'm frustrated (or bored, tired, impatient, etc.) so I'll just quit" attitude is rampant in our society.

- Working hard in school to meet academic goals is tough, so we quit.
- Sticking with a job is tedious, so we often change jobs or careers.
- Cultivating real love in marriage requires sacrifice and working through problems, so we divorce.
- Bible study is time consuming, so we neglect it and become biblically illiterate.
- Prayer requires personal discipline, so we practice it sporadically.
- Changing attitudes challenges our thinking, so we remain negative or critical.
- Serving demands sacrifice, so we remain uninvolved.

It takes strong will and determination to buck society's trends and commit oneself to not giving up when the going gets tough. But that is what separates the victors from the defeated in the Christian life.

Some lessons are learned through patient perseverance and cannot be learned anywhere else. James wrote about these valuable life lessons:

> Be patient, then, brothers, until the Lord's coming. See how the farmer waits for the land to yield its valuable crop and how patient he is for the autumn and spring rains. You too, be patient and stand firm, because the Lord's coming is near. ... Brothers, as an example of patience in the face of suffering, take the prophets who spoke in the name of the Lord. As you know, we consider blessed those who have persevered. You have heard of Job's perseverance and have seen what the Lord finally brought about. The Lord is full of compassion and mercy (James 5:7-8, 10-12).

James is saying that problems are not meant to discourage, depress or defeat you – they are intended to develop you! So, "Let us not become weary in doing good, for at the proper time we will reap a harvest if we do not give up" (Galatians 6:9).

Get Up When Life Knocks You Down

When a giraffe is born, the first parts to emerge are the baby giraffe's front hooves and head. Then the entire giraffe appears and tumbles 10 feet to the ground, landing on its back. Within a matter of seconds, he rolls over and stands, struggling with those untried tall legs.

The mother giraffe positions herself directly over her newborn, swings her long leg outward and kicks that baby, sending it sprawling. If it doesn't get up, she kicks it all over again. If it grows tired, she kicks it again to stimulate its efforts to stand.

Each time the baby giraffe manages to get to its feet, its mother kicks it once again. Now that may seem cruel to you, but there is a reason for it. The mother is simply preparing that baby for survival, because that little giraffe must learn to get up quickly and run with the herd when danger comes, or he will not survive.

We have to learn the same lesson that baby giraffe learns, and that is when life kicks you and knocks you down, you have to get back up and not give up. Our very survival may be dependent upon our perseverance: "Blessed is the man who perseveres under trial, because when he has stood the test, he will receive the crown of life that God has promised to those who love him" (James 1:12).

Satan would love nothing better than for you to throw in the towel and just give up on faith, God, Christ and the church. In fact, that's his primary mission – to get you to quit short of the goal of salvation. He wants you to have maximum frustration and minimum perseverance. Don't let him get to you and deceive you! Determine that you will not give up, you will not quit doing God's will for your life!

We are like one of the two frogs described by the anonymous poet:

Two frogs fell into a can of cream,
Or so I've heard it told.
The sides of the can were shiny and steep,
The cream was deep and cold.

"Oh, what's the use," said one,
"Tis fate no help's around.
Goodbye my friend, goodbye sad world,"
and weeping still he drowned.
But frog number two, of sterner stuff,
dogpaddled in surprise,
But while he wiped his creamy face
and dried his creamy eyes.
"I'll swim awhile at least," he said,
or so I've heard it said.
"It really wouldn't help the world,
if one more frog were dead!"
An hour or two he kicked and swam,
Not once he stopped to mutter,
But he kicked and kicked, and swam and kicked,
And hopped out via butter!

Frog No. 2 persevered and worked so hard that he made something he could use to get out of his mess. That is what God calls us to do.

Therefore, since we are surrounded by such a great cloud of witnesses, let us throw off everything that hinders and the sin that so easily entangles, and let us run with perseverance the race marked out for us (Hebrews 12:1).

The ultimate model of perseverance was Jesus Christ. In fact, the next two verses point us to Him as our role model for not giving up:

Let us fix our eyes on Jesus, the author and perfecter of our faith, who for the joy set before him endured the cross, scorning its shame, and sat down at the right hand of the throne of God. Consider him who endured such opposition from sinful men, so that you will not grow weary and lose heart (Hebrews 12:2-3).

Jesus Christ didn't quit! He endured the mock trials, the beating, the taunting, the rejection, the lies, the loneliness, and the sins of all mankind weighing down on His shoulders at the cross – and He didn't quit!

Nobody Admires Quitters

I heard about a teenage boy who was so frustrated by school that he wanted to drop out. His dad was trying hard to encourage him not to quit: "Son, you can't quit. All great people who are remembered in history didn't quit. George Washington didn't quit. Abraham Lincoln didn't quit. Thomas Edison didn't quit. Martin Luther King Jr. didn't quit. And then there's Elmo McCringle."

The son said, "Dad, wait a minute. Who in the world is Elmo McCringle?"

The dad replied, "See, you don't remember him. He quit!"

We often don't remember the quitters, those who gave up too easily or too early. In fact, the quitters we do remember, we often hold in contempt. For example, among Jesus' disciples, who is remembered warmly, Peter or Judas?

Both Peter and Judas were among Jesus' closest earthly followers and friends, the 12 disciples. Both spent three years watching Him perform miracles and teach as One sent from God. And both failed Jesus miserably when He needed them most: Judas betrayed Him (Matthew 26:14-16, 47-50), and Peter denied Him (Matthew 26:69-75).

The difference in the way we remember these two disciples is in what happened next – Judas quit on Jesus and on life, committing suicide (Matthew 27:3-5). Peter repented and refused to give up on Jesus or on life, and went on to become a dynamic leader in the early church.

The message is clear – when you mess up of your own free will or when life throws you a curveball, don't give up – instead get up and keep going for the Lord!

Finish the Race

The 1968 Mexico City Olympic Games gave us a memorable moment that defines perseverance. The marathon is perhaps the most grueling event of the Olympics. A large number of well-conditioned distance runners from almost every continent gathered at the starting line. The gun sounded and the 26-mile race was underway. The race wound through the streets of Mexico City and concluded in Olympic Stadium. Millions of TV viewers joined the crowd in the full stadium in watching the runners cross the finish line.

The awards ceremony, as always, was inspiring. The bronze medal was presented, then the silver, and finally the gold medal was draped around the neck of the winner as he stood atop the highest platform. Marno Wolde of Ethiopia stood proudly as the national anthem of his country was played and the flag of his country was raised.

Long after the award ceremony had concluded and people had turned their attention to other events taking place in the stadium, a murmur spread through the crowd. People in the stadium slowly began to realize that the marathon was not over. A runner was still on the course.

All the other marathoners had finished more than an hour earlier. But now, a young runner named John Stephen Akhwari from the African nation of Tanzania, hobbled his way into the tunnel and onto the track, limping his way toward the finish line. He was obviously in tremendous pain. It was easy to see it in his face and also in the awkward way he was forcing himself to continue running.

He had been injured in a fall early in the race. His knees were bleeding and swollen, his leg muscles were cramping and dehydration was setting in – and yet he kept on running. Refusing to quit, he painfully crossed the finish line to the roar of the crowd and fell to the ground.

A TV reporter was finally able to tell the story of his injury a few hours later and interview the young Tanzanian about his determination to run through the pain. The reporter said, "You were injured early. You knew you could not win the race. Why didn't you stop? Why didn't you just quit?"

I love the Akhwari's answer. He said, "My country did not send me to Mexico City to start the race. They sent me to finish the race."

God did not send us here to just start the Christian life. He sent us here to persevere and finish the Christian race! Near the end of his own Christian life, his Christian race, Paul wrote:

> For I am already being poured out like a drink offering, and the time has come for my departure. I have fought the good fight, I have finished the race, I have kept the faith. Now there is in store for me the crown of righteousness, which the Lord, the righteous Judge, will award to me on that day – and not only to me, but also to all who have longed for his appearing (2 Timothy 4:6-8).

I Have Learned That...

Finish the race! Keep the faith! Don't give up and don't give in because I have learned that winners don't quit and quitters don't win!

Talking Back

1. Why do you think many people give up too easily or too quickly on their dreams?

2. Put in your own words what you think Paul is saying in Galatians 6:9.

3. Can you be patient? Can you persevere? Explain your answer.

4. What historical figures have impressed you with their example of perseverance?

5. Contrast the choices of Peter and Judas. What can we learn, good and bad, from them?

Exercising Your Faith

1. Whatever activity you are currently involved with, make a "Don't Quit" reminder for yourself:

   - Atheletes, write "Don't Quit" on your locker, shoes, etc.
   - Students, write "Don't Quit" inside your school notebook.
   - Musicians, put "Don't Quit" inside your instrument case.

2. Look for stories of people who wouldn't give up in the face of incredible odds to inspire you to not give up. Memorize Galatians 6:9 as a prayer of your heart.

Nothing Is More Important Than Personal Salvation – Nothing!

When you think of spiritual teachers, chances are the name Garth Brooks would never come to mind. Brooks was the leading sales music artist in all categories of music in the 1990s; and although most of his songs are rowdy country songs, occassionally he delivers deep personal messages in his music, perhaps even spiritual messages.

The song "Unanswered Prayers" beautifully describes God looking out for us and giving us what is best for us in answer to prayer, although we may not see it at the time. Songs like "The River" and "The Dance" are eloquent in challenging people to live life to the fullest.

One of Brooks' earliest hits was "If Tomorrow Never Comes," a haunting reminder to tell the important people in your life that you love them while you still have opportunity.

What if tomorrow never comes? What if your plans were left incomplete and your hopes unrealized because there was no tomorrow? James asked and answered this question:

> Now listen, you who say, "Today or tomorrow we will go to this or that city, spend a year there, carry on business and make money." Why, you do not even know what will happen tomorrow. What is your life? You are a mist that appears for a little while and then vanishes. Instead, you ought to say, "If

it is the Lord's will, we will live and do this or that." As it is, you boast and brag. All such boasting is evil. Anyone, then, who knows the good he ought to do and doesn't do it, sins (James 4:13-17).

James' point here is not that it is unwise to plan for our future, but it is unwise to plan a future without God! He then asks one of the most profound and probing questions in the Bible: "What is your life?" Life, our most precious gift, is loaned to us by God, and it can be short: "You are a mist that appears for a little while and then vanishes." And, of course, the obvious question at that point is: "What then?"

Quite simply, if you live without faith and obedience to God, you will die without faith and without God, as a mist that vanishes into eternal judgment. But, if you live in faith and obedience to God, your soul will live forever in the glory of heaven.

This, then, is truly the most important life lesson of all.

How Does One Become a Christian?

I was 18 years old, it was springtime, and I was a student at David Lipscomb University. As I studied the Bible with friends, I became convicted concerning the New Testament teachings of faith, repentance and baptism for the forgiveness of sins. One Tuesday night, my youth minister and three friends went to a church building in Nashville, and I confessed Jesus as Lord and was buried with Him in baptism. Even now, as I write these words, the memory of that moment is fresh in my mind. I was a brand new creation in Christ – all my sins were forgiven, and I was a Christian, a member of Jesus' church.

The Bible teaches that four distinct changes happen during the course of one's conversion to Jesus Christ: a change of heart, a change of life, a change of Lord, and a change of relationship.

The Bible also pinpoints four distinct actions that produce these changes: faith changes the heart; repentance changes the lifestyle; confession changes the Lord; and baptism changes the relationship to God. None can take the place of the other as a part of our obedience to God and becoming a Christian. Let's take a closer look at each of these actions.

■ *To become a Christian, a person must experience a change of heart produced by faith.* True faith is not inherited. Each person must come to his or her own faith in God and faith in Jesus as the Son of God. Each person must have his or her own heart changed by faith. God requires faith as the first prerequisite of becoming a Christian:

> And without faith it is impossible to please God, because anyone who comes to him must believe that he exists and that he rewards those who earnestly seek him (Hebrews 11:6).

> I have declared to both Jews and Greeks that they must turn to God in repentance and have faith in our Lord Jesus (Acts 20:21).

> For God so loved the world that He gave His only begotten Son, that whoever believes in Him should not perish but have everlasting life. For God did not send His Son into the world to condemn the world, but that the world through Him might be saved. He who believes in Him is not condemned; but he who does not believe is condemned already, because he has not believed in the name of the only begotten Son of God (John 3:16-18 NKJV).

Our hearts are changed by faith. But is that all that is required to become a Christian? Some might say, "Yes," but the Bible says there is more.

■ *To become a Christian, a person must experience a change of lifestyle produced by repentance.* A Gallup Poll sometime ago revealed that 98 percent of Americans believe in God; in other words, they had some measure of faith. But only 38 percent of those same people in the same poll said that their faith made any real difference in their lives! They conducted their lives as if God didn't exist. Would you say they were really Christians?

Being a Christian demands a change of lifestyle. This change is produced by repentance. The word repentance means "to turn." When we become a Christian, we turn from the old life of sin to a new life of faith and grace: "Therefore, if anyone is in Christ, he is a new creation; the old has gone, the new has come!" (2 Corinthians 5:17).

Our repentance and change of lifestyle must be genuine and heartfelt. We can't be like the two men who were lost on a raft in the open sea. One of them, frightened, began to pray, "O Lord, I've broken most of the commandments but now I repent. I've got some pretty bad habits – I drink, I curse, I steal, I treat people like dirt. But if my life is spared now, I promise you that I'll change, that I'll never again curse, that I'll never again … .'' Suddenly his friend yelled out to him, "Wait. Don't say another word. I think I see a ship coming toward us!"

That won't cut it! To become a Christian, one must repent and change his or her lifestyle – the old lifestyle must go, the new lifestyle must come and stay!

Our lifestyle is changed by repentance. But is that all that is required to become a Christian? No, the Bible says there is more.

■ *To become a Christian, a person must experience a change in the Lordship of his life produced by a confession in Jesus as Lord.* There is power in speaking our beliefs. Public confession shows the sincerity of our conversion and gives emphasis to our personal accountability before the Lord and other people. God demands this confession:

> That if you confess with your mouth, "Jesus is Lord," and believe in your heart that God raised him from the dead, you will be saved. For it is with your heart that you believe and are justified, and it is with your mouth that you confess and are saved (Romans 10:9-10).

> "Whoever acknowledges [confesses] me before men, I will also acknowledge him before my father in heaven. But whoever disowns me before men, I will disown him before my father in heaven" (Matthew 10:32-33).

These scriptures make it clear that confessing Jesus as Lord is essential for becoming a Christian. But are we a Christian when we have faith in Jesus, repent or change our lifestyle, and publicly confess Jesus as Lord? Some might say "yes," but the Bible teaches there is still more to do.

■ *To become a Christian, a person must change his relationship with God through baptism.* Baptism doesn't change the heart or the lifestyle, but God designed baptism to change our relationship with Him. Understanding the proper roles of faith, repentance, confession and baptism will clear up many of the misunderstandings about conversion to Christ.

Have you ever known a wonderful and kind person who has never been baptized? Have you ever known a person who has been baptized but still lives a very sinful lifestyle? You see, baptism doesn't produce faith and it doesn't produce a changed lifestyle. If a person is baptized whose heart has not been changed by faith and whose lifestyle has not been changed by repentance, he will be no better after baptism than before baptism – because the purpose of baptism is to change the relationship with God! Baptism is the occasion where the relationship with God changes and our sins are washed away! Baptism will not do what faith, repentance, and confession were designed by God to do and faith, repentance and confession will not do what God designed baptism to do.

When the church began on the Day of Pentecost in Acts 2, Peter made these distinctions clear:

> "Therefore let all Israel be assured of this: God has made this Jesus, whom you crucified, both Lord and Christ." When the people heard this, they were cut to the heart and said to Peter and the other apostles, "Brothers, what shall we do?" Peter replied, "Repent and be baptized, every one of you, in the name of Jesus Christ for the forgiveness of your sins. And you will receive the gift of the Holy Spirit" (Acts 2:36-38).

Clearly these people who asked, "What shall we do?" believed the message that Jesus was the Savior, and they were "cut to the heart" (that is, their hearts were being changed by faith), but there was still more to do in order to become a Christian. They were told to "[r]epent and be baptized ... for the forgiveness of your sins."

Faith had changed their hearts but not their relationship to God. Faith had changed their hearts but their sins were not washed away and forgiven.

Becoming a Christian is not an either/or proposition. It is not faith or baptism. It is faith and baptism. It is not repentance or baptism. It is repentance and baptism. It is not confession or baptism It is confession and baptism. The reason is ...

- Faith changes the heart, but not the lifestyle, the Lord, or the relationship.
- Repentance changes the lifestyle, but not the heart, the Lord, or the relationship.

- Confession changes the acknowledgement of what or who is Lord of your life, but it doesn't change your heart, your lifestyle, or your relationship with the Lord.
- Baptism changes your relationship with the Lord and is the occasion where your sins are washed away, but it doesn't change the heart or the lifestyle.

Understanding the Roles of Faith, Repentance, Confession and Baptism

We must come to a proper understanding of the biblical roles and reasons for faith, repentance, confession and baptism. In my book, *Basic Training: A Manual for Teens*, I used this illustration to help understand these roles:

I knew my wife several months before we ever started dating. We liked each other as friends, but both of us were dating other people and had no unifying commitment to one another. As time progressed, we began dating and spending a lot of time together, eventually falling in love.

Were we married at this point? Of course not. The relationship had not yet been changed by the occasion of a wedding ceremony.

Over the course of several months, we stopped dating other people and became engaged. Certainly we believed in one another and had experienced a change of heart about ourselves and others – and, of course, a change of lifestyle was apparent.

Were we married yet? No, a change of lifestyle and priorities are essential to a good marriage, but they don't mean you are married.

Our wedding date finally arrived, and the wedding ceremony was performed. We repeated our vows, exchanged rings, and were pronounced husband and wife.

Were we married yet? Yes!

We weren't married when our hearts changed, when we fell in love and believed in one another as future life partners (that's faith or belief). We weren't married when our lifestyles and priorities changed (that's repentance). We were married on the occasion when our relationship toward one another changed (that's baptism).

We must not allow the roles and purposes of faith, repentance, confession and baptism to be confused. To become a Christian, a person must change his or her heart (through faith), change his or her lifestyle (through repentance), change his or her Lord (through confession), and change his or her relationship to God and have his or her sins washed away and forgiven (that's baptism).

What Is Your Eternal Destination?

The reason these truths are so important, the most important life lesson, is simple: All people are heading for either heaven or hell for eternity. No issue is more important than personal salvation – going to heaven and not hell!

I wish the Bible didn't say anything about hell. I wish the Bible said that if you reject Jesus Christ and you die, that's it, you just dissolve into nothingness. But the Bible teaches that hell is a place of eternal punishment for those who don't obey the Lord (Matthew 5:21-30; 25:31-46; Luke16:19-31; Revelation 20:10-15).

Hell wasn't really created for people. It was created as a place of punishment for Satan and his angels:

> And the devil, who deceived them, was thrown into the lake of burning sulfur, where the beast and the false prophet had been thrown. They will be tormented day and night for ever and ever (Revelation 20:10).

But, if we choose to reject God and say, "I don't want you, I don't want your Son, I don't want the church, I don't want your standards," God will respect your free-will choice and let you go your own way. But beware of the consequence of that choice:

> Then death and Hades were thrown into the lake of fire. The lake of fire is the second death. If anyone's name was not found written in the book of life, he was thrown into the lake of fire (Revelation 20:14-15).

The great news is the Christian who obeys God doesn't have to worry about hell after death. Christians have been promised the exact opposite of hell, an eternity in heaven.

> Then I saw a new heaven and a new earth, for the first heaven and the first earth had passed away, and there was no longer any

sea. I saw the Holy City, the new Jerusalem, coming down out
of heaven from God, prepared as a bride beautifully dressed for
her husband. And I heard a loud voice from the throne saying,
"Now the dwelling of God is with men, and he will live with
them. They will be his people, and God himself will be with
them and be their God. He will wipe every tear from their eyes.
There will be no more death or mourning or crying or pain,
for the old order of things has passed away (Revelation 21:1-4).

The choice is clear: obedience or disobedience – heaven or hell!

Personal Salvation Is a Priority

In 1997, I went through a one-year journey that taught me more about
the priority of personal salvation than any other experience I've ever
faced in my ministry. Michelle was a bright-eyed, enthusiastic, upbeat
21-year old-lady. Members of her family were in my congregation, but
Michelle had never become a Christian and only attended sporadically.

Michelle was a single mom and doted on her beautiful little girl. She
had made mistakes in her past, but was trying to get her life together
and be a good mother when suddenly pain hit her lower abdomen. After
several trips to the doctor, x-rays and ultrasound, the diagnosis was in
– a rare and very serious form of leukemia.

For several weeks, Michelle underwent various forms of drug treatment, including chemotherapy, but the disease continued to spread. Still
Michelle's spirit and optimism stayed strong. I noticed she was at church
more often.

On two or three occasions, I asked Michelle if we could study the
Bible together and discuss God's will for her, but she would always put
me off. Other people, realizing the serious nature of her disease, made
the same request and got the same response.

Finally, one Sunday I preached a strong message about personal salvation, and I was convicted after the service to approach Michelle even
more forcefully about the condition of her eternal soul. I pulled her,
along with her sister, aside and made the same offer to study, and, once
again, she stalled and tried to put it off. As tears welled up in my eyes
I said, "Michelle, I don't want to push you, and I think you know that.

But this is the most important decision, the most important choice, with the most significant consequences, that you will ever make. Please, please think seriously about it." Michelle blurted out, "Can you baptize me tonight?" Could I? I had been praying, her family had been praying, most of the church had been praying for that response!

Less than a month later, Michelle was sent to a hospital 130 miles away for a bone-marrow transplant, which required three months of confinement in a hospital room. Visitors had to wash thoroughly and put on protective clothing to visit her. I will never forget my first visit to her hospital room. Michelle was in bed, very weak, had lost all her hair, but had lost nothing of her spirit and optimism. I think she ministered more to me than I did to her!

As I looked above her bed, there were several pictures taped to the wall – some of her family and friends, some of her beautiful 2-year-old daughter, and one of her baptism just a few weeks earlier. I asked her about the pictures and as she pointed to the one of her baptism, she said, "That was the happiest moment of my life. I knew that night that no matter what happens to me physically, I will live forever in heaven."

I wish I could tell you the story had a happy ending. Michelle kept her sweet smile and strong spirit right to the end six months later. As I visited her hospital room three hours before she died, she mustered up every ounce of strength she had to lean up on one arm and hug me … and then she said, "Thank you for everything." I knew what she was saying: "Thank you for sharing the gospel."

Michelle's mother gave me the picture of her baptism that hung on the wall of her hospital room. Every time I go out of town to preach I put it in my pocket to remind me of the ultimate priority of doing everything within my power to share the saving gospel of Jesus Christ with people. It makes all the difference in the world – the difference between eternal life and eternal death, the difference between heaven and hell.

I Have Learned That...

So, the most important real life lesson I've learned is this: Nothing is more important than personal salvation – nothing!

Talking Back

1. How would you answer the question of James 4, "What is your life?"

2. How would you define faith? What is its role?

3. How would you define repentance? What is its role?

4. How would you define baptism? What is its role?

5. If you have become a Christian by faith, repentance and baptism, what does it mean to you? How has it changed your life? If you have not yet become a Christian, why not?

Exercising Your Faith

1. If you have a friend who is not a Christian, write a letter telling your friend about Jesus' love and your love for him or her. Ask your friend to study this chapter with you.

2. If you have a picture of your baptism, like Michelle, hang it up in your room or put it in your purse/wallet to remind you that your sins were washed away and you belong to God.

Also available by Randy Simmons:

Basic Training: A Manual for Teens
Thirteen lessons about basic Bible teachings that people need to know such as the Holy Spirit, faith, repentance, baptism, the church and more!

0-89225-390-8

0-89225-299-5

Straight Talk for Teens
Honest, straightforward discussion of 13 contemporary issues facing today's teenagers, based squarely on God's Word.

0-89225-423-8

What to Do When You Don't Know What to Do
A teen's guide for coping with life's problems. What do you do when you don't know what to do? Turn to the world's #1 advice provider, God.

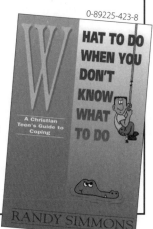

Are Your Teens
Equipped
with a
Solid Foundation?

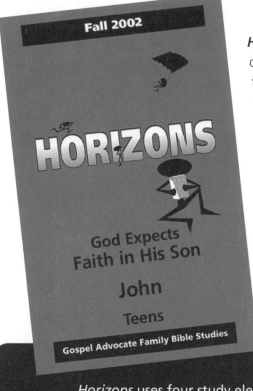

Fall 2002

HORIZONS

God Expects
Faith in His Son

John

Teens

Gospel Advocate Family Bible Studies

Horizons is a popular quarterly curriculum for teens and helps them find God's will for their lives. Its themes follow those of *Foundations*, the Gospel Advocate's adult quarterly, but *Horizons* is taught on the teen's level in ways designed to appeal especially to them.

Horizons uses four study elements –
- •Bible text based on NKJV,
- •Discussion Time,
- •Life Applications, and
- •Activities

– to reach out to teenagers and help them grow in spirit and in truth.

Available at your local Christian bookstore.

GOSPEL
ADVOCATE
A TRUSTED NAME SINCE 1855

"What Must I Do to Be Saved?"

This is the one question that *demands* a correct answer.

Because all people have sinned, God has made a way to find forgiveness.

If forgiveness is based on God's grace, how do people find that grace? Some say, "Just pray asking Jesus into your heart." Is that in the Bible? **Is baptism really necessary?**

Dan Chambers, following up on his earlier book *"Where's the Piano?"*, takes a thorough but easy-to-understand look at the Bible's teaching on salvation. He also looks at history to see what the early church understood about baptism's role in becoming a Christian.

Call your local Christian bookstore to order your copies today!

0-89225-520-X

0-89225-393-2

GOSPEL
ADVOCATE
A TRUSTED NAME SINCE 1855